METHODISM MOCKED

Frontispiece from *Sketches for Tabernacle-Frames* (1778). The 'explanation' reads: 'REYNARD *in a* Master of Arts' *Gown, with an old Fox's Head, and a* cloven Foot, *&c.*—He stands *upon three* constitutional Writers, *and* Magna Charta, *to shew his Contempt of them.*—*He is drawing the Teeth of One of his* Flock of Saints, *a working Mechanic, kneeling, with a* Jack-Ass's Head.—*Behind* Reynard *is a* Crosier, *denoting him a* Mock-Bishop.—*He is supposed to be officiating in his Shop, where he sells* Books *of* three Kinds, *viz.* Primitive Physic, Political Pamphlets, *and* Prayers, Sermons, Hymns, *etc.*—*There are two Pictures in his Shop;* one *of K.* James II. *shewing him to be a* Jacobite; *the* other *of* Lucy Cooper, *to denote him an* old Letcher.—*&c. &c. &c.*'

[*Frontispiece*

METHODISM MOCKED
*The Satiric Reaction to Methodism
in the Eighteenth Century*

ALBERT M. LYLES

WIPF & STOCK · Eugene, Oregon

Wipf and Stock Publishers
199 W 8th Ave, Suite 3
Eugene, OR 97401

Methodism Mocked
The Satiric Reaction to Methodism in the Eighteenth Century
By Lyles, Albert M.
Copyright©1960 Methodist Publishing - Epworth Press
ISBN 13: 978-1-4982-0752-2
Publication date 2/2/2015
Previously published by Epworth Press, 1960

Every effort has been made to trace the current copyright owner
of this publication but without success. If you have any information
or interest in the copyright, please contact the publishers.

TO THE MEMORY
OF MY FATHER AND MOTHER

Acknowledgements

ALTHOUGH it is impossible for me to acknowledge my indebtedness to all who have aided me in this study, I should like to express my gratitude for my most obvious debts. Professor Robert A. Aubin of Douglass College and Professor Paul Fussell of Rutgers University have given me invaluable criticism and guidance. The staffs of the following libraries have been particularly helpful: Rutgers University, Union Theological Seminary, General Theological Seminary, the University of Tennessee, Drew University, and the New York Public.

I should like also to thank Dr John C. Hodges and the English Department of the University of Tennessee for generous support. A.M.L.

Contents

Acknowledgements	6
List of Illustrations	9
Introduction	11
I The Nature of Eighteenth-century Satire and its Relation to Methodism	15
II The Attack on Methodist Enthusiasm	32
III Satire of Methodist Doctrines	44
IV Satire of Methodist Preachers and Preaching	62
V Satire of Methodist Practices	82
VI Satire of Methodist Converts and Conversion	96
VII Satire of John Wesley	111
VIII Satire of George Whitefield	127
IX Satire of Other Methodists	139
X The Methodists and the Church	149
XI The Conventions of the Satires	164
Bibliography	172
Index	187

List of Illustrations

'Toothless, he draws the Teeth of all his Flocks' *Frontispiece*

Title page from
   The Saints, A Satire   *facing page* 48

Frontispiece from
   Perfection, A Poetical Epistle   80

Frontispiece from
   The Temple of Imposture, A Poem   112

'Reynardo's Consecration by the Goddess Murcia'   144

Introduction

THE ORIGINS and development of the Methodist movement in England in the eighteenth century have been repeatedly explored, but the satiric opposition to the movement, though noticed, has not been thoroughly examined. Yet such an examination is necessary for one to understand eighteenth-century Methodism as an eighteenth-century Englishman might have seen it. In this study of the satiric reaction to Methodism I have begun with 9th December 1732, the date of the publication of the first known attack on the Methodists in *Fogg's Weekly Journal*, and ended arbitrarily at 1800 to limit the study to the eighteenth century. I have permitted myself only one exception: George Crabbe's *The Borough*, although published in 1810, has been included because of its literary merit.

Within these limits, 1732–1800, the study was intended to be exhaustive. But it soon became obvious that completeness was more to be desired than readily attained, since even the earliest chroniclers of anti-Methodist writing had been unable to examine all of it.[1] In some cases they had seen only advertisements for items which were obviously satiric. Later writers, like T. B. Shepherd, in *Methodism and the Literature of the Eighteenth Century* (1947), have been more concerned with the literature written by Methodists; Josiah Henry Barr, in *Early Methodists under Persecution* (1916), studies only a minute portion of the satires. An exhaustive examination of distinct satires and of the vast body of anti-Methodist satire in letters, journals, and minor non-satiric works would be impossible.

---

[1] See particularly [Curtis H. Cavender] *Catalogue of Works in Refutation of Methodism, from Its Origin in 1729, to the Present Time* (Philadelphia, 1846); Richard Green, *Anti-Methodist Publications Issued during the Eighteenth Century* (London, 1902); Luke Tyerman, *The Life and Times of the Rev. John Wesley, M.A., Founder of the Methodists* (6th edn, London, 1890), and Tyerman, *The Life of the Rev. George Whitefield* (London, 1876–7).

INTRODUCTION

The term *satire* is defined loosely. It is used as a generic rather than a specific term. Within it, for purposes of this study, are included the burlesque, the lampoon, the mock heroic, the parody, ironic statements, and occasionally invective designed simply for ridicule of its victim.

The satiric material itself has been arranged in categories such as satire of Methodist doctrines, satire of Methodist practices, satire of Methodist conversion, and satire of individual Methodists. Such a scheme will permit the consideration of satiric references to Methodism from works not devoted primarily to satire or to Methodism. Such references form a considerable portion of the satiric depiction of Methodism. The prevalence of such references indeed prevents the classification of the material according to the most obvious pattern, that of technical form: prose satire, Hudibrastics, blank verse, and heroic couplet. The use of such a scheme will also reveal those characteristics of Methodism and those Methodists most satirized.

Obviously the reading of satire on such a basis must be done carefully. Some of the satirists, although the number is disappointingly small, are conscious literary artists, and the resulting creation cannot be read as polemic or even solely as a pejorative depiction of reality. Exaggeration for comic or satiric effect plays an important role. One must not assume, for example, that the prevalence of satiric references to cobblers turned preachers indicated any particular animosity on the part of the satirists to cobblers, but must recognize that the easy pun, expressed or unexpressed, upon souls accounts in part for the satiric anathematizing. Yet a carefully developed categorizing of those qualities of the Methodists and those individuals satirized may lead to an understanding of the immense satiric reaction to Methodism and may also provide an insight into satiric techniques of the middle and late eighteenth century.

In examining the material, I have tried deliberately to approach the anti-Methodist position sympathetically, since only in that way can we understand many of the attacks upon

INTRODUCTION

Methodism, which has long ago demonstrated its strength and its value. Because I am concerned principally with what the satirists believed or alleged about Methodism, I have not tried to demonstrate whether a particular allegation or accusation was true or false. Where an accusation is based upon mutual misunderstanding—for example, the attack on the doctrine of assurance—I have tried to state both the Methodist and anti-Methodist positions fairly.

The long encyclopedic titles of the eighteenth-century works have been shortened in the text. The full titles can be found in the bibliography. I have cited secondary sources only when I have actually quoted directly or when I am indebted for specific information.

CHAPTER ONE

The Nature of Eighteenth-century Satire and its Relation to Methodism

EVEN BEFORE the Methodist leaders, George Whitefield and John Wesley, embarked in 1739 upon the precedent of preaching in the fields in direct violation of the Conventicle Act, they inspired a flood of attacks, satiric and non-satiric, which, although it abated occasionally, was to continue into the nineteenth century. The opposition to Methodism and the Methodist leaders reached gigantic proportions. Richard Green in his *Bibliography of Anti-Methodist Literature of the Eighteenth Century* (1902) lists 606 anti-Methodist items. Obviously many of these are non-satiric, but such a figure indicates the extent to which Methodism was attacked during the century. The attacks ranged from the first known one, the anonymous letter in *Fogg's Weekly Journal* of 9th December 1732, one paragraph of which Luke Tyerman, the Methodist historian, calls 'so loathsomely impure, that it would be a sin against both God and man to reproduce it', to the mild *Earnest and Affectionate Address to the People Called Methodists* (1745); from an apparently serious attempt to account for the conduct of George Whitefield, the Calvinist Methodist, and that 'of his unhappy, gloomy, and misguided Followers' on the basis of astronomical calculation,[1] to Punchinello shows in which Dr Squintum, one of a half-dozen terms applied by the anti-Methodists to Whitefield, harangued a group of puppets and picked their pockets as they gazed heavenward. The attacks ranged in length from Charles Wesley's term *Melchizedekians*, applied to unordained Methodist

[1] John Harman, *Remarks upon the Life, Character, and Behaviour of the Rev. George Whitefield* (London, 1764).

15

preachers,[2] to Richard Graves's two-volume novel, *The Spiritual Quixote, or, The Summer's Ramble of Mr Geoffrey Wildgoose* (1773), which Graves's biographer calls 'the literary monument of anti-Methodism'.[3]

The attacks poured forth in various forms: prose, heroic couplets, blank verse, and Hudibrastics were the main ones. Less skilful hands than those of Jonathan Swift attempted to display the mechanical operation of the Spirit in the Methodist; less successful ones than Alexander Pope's tried to reveal the secret to each Methodist ass that he was a deluded fool. Even Milton's Satan, in less sonorous verse, called upon John Wesley. But the most appropriate model for the satirist of Methodism was Samuel Butler's *Hudibras;* here the satirist saw art greater than his own attack the hypocrisy of an earlier religious enthusiasm very similar to the enthusiasm of Methodism. Thus from eighteenth-century presses poured forth Hudibrastics lampooning a new fanatic tribe. Yet the form, its representatives often subliterary, which attacked Methodism most severely was the drama. The attack was begun in *The Minor* in 1760 by Samuel Foote, who for nearly twenty years flayed the religious movement with *The Lyar* (1760), *The Orators* (1762), *The Devil upon Two Sticks* (1778), and a continuing controversy with a Methodist, probably Martin Madan. Foote's attack provided a pattern, and in 1760, the year *The Minor* was produced, appeared Joseph Reed's *The Register-Office*, using essentially the same satire, and probably in the next year was published Israel Pottinger's *The Methodist*, which its title page advertised as being a continuation of *The Minor*. Probably soon after appeared *The Spiritual Minor*, although the date of its publication is uncertain. Interestingly enough, the stage attacks were aimed primarily at Whitefield and not at his fellow-Methodist,

---

[2] Cited in Thomas Jackson, *The Life of the Rev. Charles Wesley, M.A.* (New York, 1842), p. 502.
[3] Charles Jarvis Hill, *The Literary Career of Richard Graves*, Smith College Studies in Modern Languages, Vol. XVI, Nos. 1–3 (Northampton, 1935), p. 16.

John Wesley, probably because of the flamboyance of the former.[4]

The attacks on Methodism came from all sides and probably for various reasons. The dramatists, suffering from Methodist attacks on attendance at playhouses, responded with a series of counter-attacks. Occasionally an individual attacked Methodism to indicate that he was not a Methodist. A Mrs Rich, an actress who renounced the theatre after her conversion to Methodism, wrote to one of the Wesleys on 17th November 1746: 'The enclosed is a copy of a song Mr Rich [probably John Rich, a theatre manager] has sung in a new scene added to one of his old entertainments, in the character of Harlequin Preacher, to convince the town he is not a Methodist.' Certain periodicals were anti-Methodist. Tyerman rates the *Weekly Miscellany* and the *Monthly Review* as scurrilous in their attacks.

But by far the largest group of attackers of Methodism was the established clergy. Obviously, as Josiah Henry Barr notes, the clergy were not all opposed, but many were.[5] The clerical attack was led by Dr Joseph Trapp, rector of Harlington in Sussex, and joint-lecturer at St Martin-in-the-Fields. He preached at Christ Church, Newgate Street, with Whitefield in the audience, on the text: 'Be not righteous overmuch. . . .' The series of sermons was published in 1739 as *The Nature, Folly, Sin, and Danger of Being Righteous Overmuch*.[6] Trapp found a worthy successor in George Lavington, the Bishop of Exeter, who attempted to link Methodism to Roman Catholicism in his

---

[4] T. B. Shepherd, 'Methodists and the Theatre in the Eighteenth Century', *Proceedings of the Wesley Historical Society*, XXXI (1937–8), p. 5.
[5] *Early Methodists under Persecution* (New York, 1916), p. 158.
[6] Albert D. Belden, *George Whitefield—The Awakener* (2nd edn, London, 1953), pp. 73–4. That even anti-Methodists were not unaware that this was an unlikely pitfall is evidenced by a satiric thrust at Trapp in *The Mock Preacher: a Satyrico-Comical-Allegorical Farce* (London, 1739). The chairman, who acquits the mock-preacher, says to him: 'I would not have you be a Methodist any longer, nor be over-righteous; for being over-righteous is a Sin, a very great Sin indeed—There are some Discourses printed against being over-righteous . . .' (pp. 27–8). Throughout this study I have retained all eighteenth-century punctuation and spelling since satire is often indicated in this fashion.

lengthy study, *The Enthusiasm of Methodists and Papists Compar'd* (1749). No segment of the established clergy, however, attacked Methodism more severely than the Methodists themselves. The historian Lecky says of the quarrel between the Wesleyan and Calvinist Methodists: 'Whatever calumny, whatever injustice, whatever violence of language was displayed by the enemies of Methodism, they never equalled the ferocity exhibited by the saints in their internal quarrels.'[7] Wesleyan Methodism received perhaps its severest blows from the unskilful but effective attacks of the Calvinists John MacGowan, Rowland Hill, and Augustus Toplady.

It is difficult to generalize about the period of satire. One is tempted to say that after years of active ministry by the Methodist leaders the movement grew respectable and the satiric attacks dwindled to a trickle, but such a generalization is only partially true. Wesley in his old age (1775–91) was respected and even venerated, but in 1778 five of the most vitriolic of the satires against Wesley and Methodism appeared. And although Wesley was more respected, Methodism and the Methodists were still viewed with suspicion or simply used as subjects of satire.

Yet the satire does seem to ebb and flow. The following years represent the peaks of the satire of Methodism: 1739, 1760, 1772, 1778. The significance of the 1739 satire is obvious. George Whitefield and the Wesleys had embarked upon the dangerous precedent of field preaching in direct violation of the Conventicle Act, one of the Restoration laws regulating non-Anglican worship. For the first time they preached their enthusiastic doctrine of justification by faith. While the nature of this satire will be discussed later, the extent of it may be realized when we consider Harold King's assertion that of 200 anti-Methodist publications, not simply satires, during 1739–40, 154 were aimed at George Whitefield.[8] The prevalence of satire

---

[7] W. E. H. Lecky, *A History of England in the Eighteenth Century* (new edn, New York, 1892), III.97.

[8] 'God's Dramatist', *Studies in Speech and Drama in Honor of Alexander M. Drummond* (Ithaca, 1944), p. 369.

in 1760 may be accounted for by the success of *The Minor* and its imitations. After Whitefield's death in 1770, the satire was aimed largely at Wesley. The attacks of 1771–2 mark the Calvinist reaction to Wesley's insistence at the 1770 Methodist Conference that Methodism had leaned too much toward Calvinism. The group of satires in 1778, although aimed at various things, bitterly attacks Wesley's defence of the government's position on the American colonies, a view he stated in *A Calm Address to Our American Colonies*, published in 1775.

Such, then, is the general extent of the eighteenth-century satire of Methodism. The nature and degree of that satire will be seen in subsequent chapters.

This study is concerned with only one of the weapons used by the adversaries of the Saints, satire. But for an understanding of that satire, it is necessary to reaffirm some principles of Augustan satire before examining the purpose of the anti-Methodist satirist. First, satire was the major literary achievement of the Augustans and was the characteristic response to experience. The Augustan wrote satire as naturally as later poets were to write lyrics. Yet satire was not a limited literary type. Ian Jack reminds us: 'The first step towards an understanding of Augustan satire is to realize that it is not, in the specialized sense, a poetic "kind". It is a temper of writing, unsusceptible of any but a very wide definition, which may find an outlet in any of a number of different kinds and in correspondingly diverse styles.'[9] Although the great period of eighteenth-century satire was to end with the deaths of Pope and Swift, still in 1739 the anonymous author of *The Mock-Preacher* could write: '... I was inform'd, that nothing would please the Town, but severe Satire, Bawdy, or some very smart political Piece.' Although his statement is half ironic, it nevertheless testifies to the continuing popularity of satire among the late Augustans.

Secondly, it is important to realize that eighteenth-century

[9] *Augustan Satire: Intention and Idiom in English Poetry 1660–1750* (Oxford, 1952), p. 146.

satire, although aimed at individuals, was often not intended simply as personal attack. Despite the fact that Alexander Pope wrote in the *Epistle to Dr Arbuthnot*,

> Out with it, Dunciad! Let the secret pass,
> That secret to each fool, that he's an Ass,

he at least publicly did not attack the fools simply for the purpose of attack. Behind the attack lay generally an avowed worthy purpose. Pope wrote in the same poem of a poet:

> That not for fame, but virtu's better end,
> He stood the furious foe, the timid friend.

Negatively then it is almost a commonplace to say of eighteenth-century satire that it generally was not simply personal invective. In addition, although Dr Johnson distinguished between satire and lampoon and defined the latter as 'censure written not to reform but to vex', a modern critic, Ian Jack, developing the views of Joseph Trapp, the first Oxford Professor of Poetry, shows that even the lampoon need not have spite for its motive, that its rhetoric, like that of an orator, is chosen for the effect it will have upon an audience. Positively, the vituperation of the satirist must be read as a literary device and not as a statement of his opinion.

In the third place it is necessary to recognize that eighteenth-century satire was not simply the artistic creation of a species of comedy but was also, many times, a moral judgement made by the satirist out of indignation as he saw individuals deviating from the right standards. The satirist, viewed in this manner, was a defender of right. James Sutherland has warned that we must remember that 'the satirist was deliberately reinforcing the agreed standards of the age by pointing out the eccentric, the anti-social, the freethinker, the profligate, the antinomian'.[10]

[10] *A Preface to Eighteenth-century Poetry* (Oxford, 1948, 1950), p. 39. See also Louis I. Bredvold, 'A Note in Defence of Satire', *ELH*, VII (1940), p. 259.

The satirist then placed himself on an eminence above his fellow man, saw his frailties, and ridiculed him with them certainly for the entertainment of himself and his audience but also for the avowed purpose of the improvement of society. Such a purpose, implied at least, was in the mind of Samuel Bowden, who wrote in the introduction to his 'The Mechanic Inspir'd: or, The Methodist's Welcome to *Frome*. A Ballad', in 1754: 'It may be proper to mention, that the Design of the following Song is not to lampoon the honest and sincere, but only to expose pretended Zealots, and designing Enthusiasts. Irony and Banter seem best adapted to ridicule such Visionarys, who are declared Enemies of all Reason and Learning. Those who depart from Reason become the proper objects of Satyr and Laughter.' Such was the view expressed by another satirist of Methodism, Richard Graves, in his 'Apology' for *The Spiritual Quixote:* 'The following narrative was intended to expose a species of folly which has frequently disturbed the tranquillity of this nation. The author, indeed, by no means considers ridicule as a proper test of religious opinions. . . . the following work is so far from ridiculing religion (as, perhaps, may be objected), that, he flatters himself, it has a direct tendency to prevent religion becoming ridiculous by the absurd conduct of such irregular teachers of it.'[11] An enemy to reason and learning was an enemy to society and a proper subject of satire. The person satirized would be displayed to his fellow citizens as an aberration, a deviation from the desired norm.

The first satirists of Methodism, when they derisively applied the epithet 'Methodist', had a specific group in mind, but the word later became a generic term for any kind of religious irregularity. The development of the definition of the word in the eighteenth century is an integral part of the study of the satire. The term, which was originally given as a derogatory epithet

[11] *The Spiritual Quixote, or, The Summer's Ramble of Mr Geoffrey Wildgoose*, 2 vols., intro. Charles Whibley (London, 1926), I.3-4.

because of the regularity and method of their lives[12] to a group of earnest young Oxford students who met together under the leadership of John Wesley, was soon applied to any person with pretensions of strong religious experience of any sort. The term 'Methodist' was an old one, having reference to a school of physicians under Nero who had put their patients under stringent regimens. It had perhaps even been applied to religious groups in England before the time of the eighteenth-century religious revival. Although it is probably a mistake to assume that the Methodist movement began with the Holy Club at Oxford, it is to this group of young men that that term was first applied because of the regularity of their lives.[13] The term was later applied to even the most moderate Evangelicals and indeed to anyone with the appearance of an emotional faith.[14]

How indiscriminately broad the definition had become may be seen in the statement of a cleric antagonistic to Methodism, John Downes, rector of St Michael, Ward Street. Writing in 1759 in *Methodism Examined and Disposed*, he urged that all clergy who are Methodists or are suspected of Methodism be barred from the pulpit:

I am not ignorant upon what weak and slender Grounds a Suspicion of that sort is apt to be founded.—Sometimes a Preacher unhappily incurs it by his Voice, Manner, Gestures, Pronunciation, nay, even by his very Countenance.—Sometimes by the Pathos of his Stile, and the Vehemency of his Address. ... But then sometimes again, he brings it upon himself; as by heaping Scripture upon Scripture, either foreign to his Subject,

[12] T. B. Shepherd, *Methodism and the Literature of the Eighteenth Century*, p. 15. It was only one of a group of names. Others were the Holy Club and Bible Moths.

[13] L. E. Elliott-Binns, *The Early Evangelicals: A Religious and Social Study* (London, 1953), p. 123. Elliott-Binns's argument is that the Oxford group was a group similar to many other high church groups within the Established Church in the seventeenth and eighteenth centuries. He asserts as well that the Fetter Lane Society, in which John Wesley experienced his conversion, was not Moravian but Anglican. (See p. 372.)

[14] There will be no attempt in this study to distinguish between the Evangelicals and the Methodists, since, as the discussion of the term *Methodist* will make clear, for the conservative anyone possessing certain attributes was a Methodist.

or unconnected with his Matter; by a studied and more frequent Repetition, or hackneyed use of the adorable name of Jesus, than is either prudent or decent; by being fond of rapturous Expressions, and high Flights of Piety, soaring quite beyond the Regions of Reason and Common Sense.

For the Reverend Mr Downes a Methodist must have been lurking behind every church door. An anonymous author, writing in 1781, confessed that a description of Methodism was beyond his powers but nevertheless attempted a more precise definition than that of Mr Downes: '*Pure* METHODISM, as it subsisted under its founder, WHITFIELD, and some of his immediate followers, as far as such a Scheme is capable of description, seems to place Religion wholly, or chiefly, in certain inexplicable impulses, or movements of the mind; and requires of its votaries to commit themselves to the guidance of the Spirit, with an utter contempt of reason, and all human learning.'[15] Methodism thus had become a term for a method of religious experience. The Reverend Walter Shirley, a Calvinist foe of Mr Wesley, in 1771 published an attack upon the Minutes of the Methodist Conference of the preceding year. This reveals how inclusive the term had become. This attack was necessary, he wrote: 'For as the world too frequently confounds all the Friends to vital Christianity under the common Name of *Methodists* we were solicitous, that no Imputation should lie upon our Names, either in present or future Times, as tacitly consenting to Doctrines which we apprehended were fundamentally erroneous.'

Methodists themselves were no less desirous of extending the meaning of the term and of attributing to themselves all of the religious zeal of the eighteenth century. Indeed the anti-Methodist author of *A Letter to the Reverend Mr George Whitefield* (1750) implies that the Oxford group gave the name to itself: 'If I am not misinformed, by one who was a member of your club, ye were no ways displeased at being called (if ye did not give yourselves the title of) Methodists, at your first setting

[15] *An Essay on the Character of Methodism* (Cambridge, 1781), p. 7.

up.' The ardent author of *Methodism Displayed, and Enthusiasm Detected* (1757), a well-developed defence of Methodism, glorifies the term: 'A Methodist! Why really 'tis a simple and inoffensive Name, and I don't see any Reason to be ashamed of it; for I have often thought, and it's well worth Notice, that the World don't usually fix this Appellation upon Persons of an openly wicked and scandalously sinful life: Hence a gaming, pleasure-taking, Playhouse-frequenting Person, one who lives in Debauchery and Excess of Drinking, is sure to escape the Name of Methodist.' Picking up the argument that the Methodists believed simply in the doctrines of the Church of England, an argument that the Methodists were to use time and time again and one which enraged their opponents, the author wrote: '. . . if for a steady Adherence and firm Attatchment to the Doctrines of the Church of *England*, I am accounted a *Methodist*, I am content, may I live and die a Church of England Methodist.' The anonymous *Letter to the Inhabitants of St Dunstan's in the West* (1759), attempting to herd all evangelicals within the fold of Methodism, chided: '. . . what a scandal it is to the church of *England* in these days, that if a minister is faithful in discharging his trust, and preaches the real Gospel, and dont sympathize with mankind in a dead moral discourse, but is a true ambassador for Jesus Christ, he is called a Methodist. . . .'

Evidently by the 1750's the term 'Methodist' was no longer an identifying term for a particular group but was an inclusive name, if not for all of those who took religion seriously, at least for all of those who were obviously evangelical. It may be due to the enlarging of the term that the satire increased. Certainly as Elliott-Binns has said: 'Unless we realize the vagaries and eccentricities of those who, rightly or wrongly, were lumped together as "Methodists", their [authorities' and parochial clergy's] excessive suspicions seem unwarranted.'[16] But obviously an ill-defined sprawling religious movement, a breeding-ground for charlatans and quacks, was a more open target

[16] Elliott-Binns, *The Early Evangelicals* . . ., p. 129.

THE NATURE OF EIGHTEENTH-CENTURY SATIRE

for satire than a tightly-knit, carefully regulated religious organization. Such an unregulated enthusiastic movement is what many persons in the eighteenth century considered Methodism to be. Recognizing then what the century considered a Methodist, it is time to examine the purpose of the satirist and the reasons behind his satire of Methodism.

Many writers on Methodism have clucked their tongues at the anti-Methodist attacks. With no attempt to explain the attacks, they write sadly that religion in the eighteenth century was at a low ebb and that it was fortunate that John Wesley appeared. Some have uncomprehendingly viewed the opponents of Methodism, particularly the satirists, as moved by spite, hatred, and even malevolence. Such a view supposes a belief in opposition simply for opposition's sake. Though undoubtedly some satirists may have been moved to write simply for delight in the rhetoric of ridicule and others by a lack of comprehension of the movement, many anti-Methodists attacked because they feared that Christianity was menaced from within.

Some of the satirists, at least, although they may have failed to perceive Methodism to be a revitalizing force in the Church, were not moved simply by malevolence and spite; they saw in Methodism serious dangers to the welfare of religion in England. While it is unsafe to generalize on the motives which lie behind an author's use of a particular rhetoric, in order to see the satire of Methodism as more than the outpourings of personal spite, it is necessary to recognize both the avowed and unavowed purposes of the satire. Undoubtedly the purposes of the anti-Methodists in satirizing were varied. They ranged from a desire to amuse or a desire for revenge to an attempt to reclaim the deluded members of the fanatic tribe. If one purpose were to be assembled from the avowed purposes of the satirists of Methodism, it would be to hold up to ridicule what the satirist considered a dangerous group of fanatics who were determined for various reasons—personal gain, insanity, and the like—to overthrow the Established Church and the Protestant faith. Although the satirists of Methodism attacked the movement on many fronts, they asserted that Methodism presented essentially five dangers: (1) the Methodists offered an easy but false way to salvation; (2) Methodists caused dissension and schism in the Church; (3) the Methodists were deliberate hypocrites; (4) the Methodists were reviving religious fanaticism; and (5) the Methodists were Papists and Jacobites (supporters of the Stuart pretender to the throne) in disguise.

First, to the uncritical eye it seems astounding that eighteenth-century Methodism can be considered to offer an easy way to heaven. In contrast to many eighteenth-century Britons here were individuals who led rigorous, God-fearing lives, who dressed plainly, who attended religious meetings at every opportunity, and who often were obliged to reveal, if they were serious Methodists, their innermost thoughts and temptations to fellow Methodists. The regularity of their lives, on Sundays particularly, was satirized by James Lackington, a former Methodist, who wrote of his wife and himself in his memoirs: 'We will still attend the preaching at five o'clock in the morning; at eight go to the prayer meeting; at ten to the public worship at the foundry; hear Mr Perry at Cripplegate, at two; be at the preaching at the Foundry, at five; meet with the general Society at six; meet in the united bands at seven and again be at the prayer meeting at eight; and then come home and read and pray by ourselves.' But to the eighteenth-century mind the Methodist insistence upon such doctrines as justification by faith, assurance, and perfection made Methodism, in terms of the title of one of the satires, a plain and easy road to the land of bliss. And the doctrine which most horrified the orthodox, even though the Articles of Religion expressly stated it, was justification by faith. Probably few members of the Church of England would question the premise that they were to be saved by Christ's merits rather than their own, but they saw perhaps too clearly that an exaggerated insistence on salvation solely by faith detracted from the concept of the value of good works. The denigration of good works in turn really emphasized a totally different view: that evil works did not matter because grace alone was the means of salvation. This the orthodox believer saw and revolted from in horror. For him Methodism was a device by which one might sin, repent, be converted, sin again, and follow the pattern *ad infinitum*. The conservative mind thus saw Methodism as a real threat to Christianity; if it was not actually antinomianism, it led to it. John Harman, the astronomer who sought to account for George Whitefield's life through the baleful influence of the stars, warned that Whitefield's ministrations were too easy: '... and as to what he [Whitefield] says, that there are as many ways to heaven as there are doors to his chapel, he might as well have said, there were as many ways there as there are sands in the sea; this, no doubt, he learnt from being inspired, for I am sure there is no text in any part of the scriptures which informs us of more than one way to heaven; as to the Methodist way, I think not the least about theirs, God forbid that I should, for I firmly believe that it has carried to the brink of hell the souls of many....' That Methodism was misleading those who should be leading sober and righteous lives many anti-Methodists feared. The author of *The Methodist, a Poem* (1766) asserted that Methodists were 'Soldiers for Hell's Church Militant'.

The second danger that the critics of Methodism saw was that the Methodists, although they claimed to be members of the Church of England, were causing dissension and schism within the Church. The Methodists asserted themselves to be true ministers of the Church and defenders of its doctrines, and at the same time they attacked its priests. Few actions of the Methodists caused so much reaction. Many supporters flew to the aid of the Church. In many cases the attackers of Methodism and the defenders of the Church became the same.

Much of the dissension was caused by the Methodist practice of sending out unordained laymen to preach the Word of God; this, in Protestant England, was considered unwarranted. The ordained Methodist, though even he was sometimes treated with contempt by the parish priest, was conservatism itself compared with the lay preacher. Lecky describes the actions of such a preacher in these words: 'The Methodist preacher came to an Anglican parish in the spirit, and with the language, of a missionary going to the most ignorant heathens; and he asked the clergyman of the parish to lend him his pulpit, in order that he might instruct the parishioners—perhaps for the first time—in the true Gospel of Christ.' Richard Graves was moved to write *The Spiritual Quixote* by the fact that a journeyman-shoemaker came into his parish with a large number of adherents, preached, won over most of Graves's congregation, and treated Graves with contempt.[17] Although Graves himself made his ideal priest in *The Spiritual Quixote*, Dr Greville, praise the work of the Wesleys, Greville added that after the Wesleys' death the Church would suffer: 'So that after prejudicing the people against their proper pastors, they will leave them a prey to ignorance, and, perhaps, much greater immorality, of illiterate plebians, and so will have made another schism in our church, to very little purpose.' That Methodism had harmed the Church William Dodd, who was later to be executed for forgery, in 1761 admitted, but he indicated how the harm could be remedied: 'Let Mr *Wesley* and Mr *Whitefield* by true Repentence undo as much as they can the Evil they had done; let them call in and disclaim their Lay-Preachers: and reconcile themselves to their Bishop and their Church: And laying aside *Assurance* and *Perfection*, let them retain all the noble Zeal and Fortitude in the Propagation of reasonable Christianity, which they have shewn in propagating Enthusiasm, and supporting a Sect.'[18] The anti-Methodists then were seriously concerned about the effect of Methodism on the Church.

A third danger that the anti-Methodists saw in Methodism,

---

[17] C. J. Hill, *The Literary Career of Richard Graves*, pp. 23–4.
[18] *A Conference between a Mystic, an Hutchinsonian, a Calvinist, a Methodist, a Member of the Church of England, and Others* (London, 1761), p. 98. Dodd included the work in the list of his works prepared as he awaited execution in 1776.

one that may account in part for the bitterness of the satire, was what they considered its hypocrisy. Some writers felt that the Methodists were charlatans who practiced a pseudo-religion for their own ends. The very claim of the Methodists that they lived according to the dictates of the Holy Spirit was evidence enough of their hypocrisy.[19] Some of the satirists of Methodism used Methodist hypocrisy as a justification for their satire. The author of *Sketches for Tabernacle-Frames* (1778), one of the bitterest of the attacks on Methodism, wrote in his 'advertisement': '... this *Tribe* of *Mock-Saints* (but especially their *Leaders*) wrest and torture *Scripture* to their own *worldly Purposes*, and substitute various *false Doctrines* (favourable to their own *Designs*) instead of *moral Honesty, Integrity, Truth*, and the plain and clear Import of the holy Scriptures. Such *pious Imposters* the *Author* treats as *lawful Game*.'

The fourth danger that some anti-Methodists saw was a fearful one: religious war. They remembered the religious fanaticism of the preceding century. They saw in Methodism the same flame that had swept throughout the country under the Puritans. The possibility of another bloody revolution was terrifying. That this was a fear even later in the century can be seen in *Methodism and Popery Dissected and Compared* (1779), when the anonymous author wrote: '... to go no farther than the *Annals* of our own Country, the hatred and bloodshed which the differences in religion have caused in Society, are sufficient to make us execrate the designing, malevolent authors of such misery, and call down the vengeance of Heaven on the future stimulators of such divisions.' Henry Carey, the author of *Sally in Our Alley*, in 'The Methodist Parson', warned:

> In religion, as well as in physick, we find
> That quacks have the art of bamboozling mankind.
> The age is roll'd round o'er a new forty-one
> 'Tis high time that new sectaries should be begun.[20]

[19] This idea will be developed in detail in Chapter 2.
[20] *The Poems of Henry Carey*, ed. Frederick T. Wood (London [1930]), p. 87.

The pseudonymous Peter Paragraph in *The Methodist and Mimick* (1767) had put into words what the eighteenth century feared of Methodism:

> *Cromwell* like you did first pretend,
> Religion was his only End;
> But soon the Mask away did fling,
> *Pull'd down the Church*, and *kill'd the King*.

Finally the anti-Methodists ironically enough saw in Methodism the danger of a return of Roman Catholicism and the Pretender to England. This danger became more obvious after 1745 when the Pretender made religion as political as it had been in the sixteenth and seventeenth centuries. On 19th July 1746, Charles Wesley wrote in his *Journal*: 'All manner of evil they say of us. Papists we are; that is certain, and are bringing in the Pretender. Nay, the vulgar are persuaded I have brought him with me; and James Waller is the man.' A charge of treason was actually preferred against Charles Wesley, and the judge before whom Wesley voluntarily went said, according to Charles's *Journal*, that 'he was informed that we constantly prayed for the pretender in all our societies....'[21] With the defeat of the Pretender in 1746, the Methodists were comparatively free at least of this charge.

Satire of Methodism then in various literary genres extended throughout the eighteenth century. Although the satire reflected various literary and social levels as well, much of it was written by the clergy, Anglican and Methodist, who in their zeal to defend their own theological position and practices and to ridicule those of their opponents were still careful to depict themselves, in the tradition of eighteenth-century satire, as defenders of the right. From the first application of the term '*Methodist*' to the group of young men at Oxford under Wesley, the meaning of the word gradually expanded to include anyone with an

---

[21] Cited in Jackson, *The Life of the Rev. Charles Wesley*, pp. 345, 296, 299. Waller was another preacher.

emotional faith. Thus the way was paved for all who, in the satirist's eyes, deviated from proper theological paths to be branded as Methodists. The satirist saw in Methodism specific dangers to the nation, the Church of England, and Christianity, or at least he used these as justification of his satire. In brief, against what it considered the error of Methodism, a deviation from the norm in religion, the eighteenth century raised the rod of satire with which it had lashed dunces in scholarship and literature.

CHAPTER TWO

The Attack on Methodist Enthusiasm

THE MOST general charge that the eighteenth century levelled against the Methodists was that of enthusiasm. The charge of enthusiasm was also one of the most serious since behind it lay the association of the Methodists with Cromwell's Puritans and with other evangelical and religiously occult groups of the late seventeenth and early eighteenth centuries, like the Quakers and the French Prophets. The eighteenth-century reader may have remembered, as he heard the charge of enthusiasm, Dryden's attack on the Puritans in *Absalom and Achitophel*:

> A numerous host of dreaming saints succeed,
> Of the true old Enthusiastic breed:
> 'Gainst form and order they their pow'r employ
> Nothing to build, and all things to destroy.

As he watched the startling conversions of the Methodists, the older and more conservative man in 1739 might well have remembered the frenzies of the French Prophets, who, in London in the reign of Queen Anne, attributed incoherent babbling to the Holy Spirit. He might well have not distinguished between their enthusiasm and that of the Methodists. But more importantly the eighteenth-century reader, when he heard the charge of enthusiasm, would almost automatically assume a deliberate hypocrisy on the part of the Methodists.

In considering this charge of enthusiasm, particularly as it appears in the satires where an outraged name-caller may simply hurl the grenade and duck behind anonymity, one needs to see what the eighteenth-century reader might have understood by the term.

Eighteenth-century religious enthusiasm obviously had roots which reached far beyond the century. The word 'enthusiasm' in its Greek origin meant inspiration by a god and as generally understood was concerned with impulses, commands, and the like coming from the gods to man.[1] In Christianity it centres upon the Pentecostal experience; indeed, as Ronald Knox asserts: 'All enthusiastic movements are fain to revive in a more or less degree, the experience of Pentecost; a new outpouring of the Holy Spirit has taken place, and a chosen body of witnesses is there to attest to it.'[2] The word 'enthusiasm' itself, then, in a Christian sense, viewed as objectively as possible, is concerned with the inspiration of the Holy Spirit. But essentially, for the eighteenth century enthusiasm meant claiming, without authority, extraordinary powers from the Holy Spirit.[3] John Locke, upon whose thought consciously or unconsciously the eighteenth century based many of its assumptions, declared in the *Essay Concerning Human Understanding* that some men, believing naturally that God can reveal Himself to men, are apt to pretend to revelation when they cannot account for their opinion by reason: 'Their minds being thus prepared, whatever groundless opinion comes to settle itself strongly upon their fancies, is an illumination from the Spirit of God, and presently of divine authority: and whatsoever odd act they find in themselves a strong inclination to do, that impulse is concluded to be a call or direction from heaven, and must be obeyed. . . .' This Locke calls enthusiasm. Dr Johnson defined it as 'A vain belief of private revelation; a vain confidence of divine favour or communication.' Joseph Trapp, one of the earliest opponents of Methodism, wrote in 1739: 'By *Enthusiasm* is meant a Person's having a strong, but false Persuasion, that he is *divinely inspired;* or at least, that he has the *Spirit of God some* way or *other;* and

[1] See M. Kevin Whalen, *Enthusiasm in English Poetry of the Eighteenth Century (1700–74)* (Washington, 1935), p. 1, and Umphrey Lee, *The Historical Backgrounds of Early Methodist Enthusiasm* (New York, 1931), pp. 16–17.
[2] *Enthusiasm, a Chapter in the History of Religion* (New York, 1951), p. 550.
[3] W. K. Lowther Clarke, *Eighteenth-century Piety* (London, 1944), p. 25.

This made known to him in a particular and *extraordinary* manner.' Religious enthusiasm in the eighteenth century can be defined generally then as a false belief in inspiration.

It was looked upon almost unanimously with suspicion. It was a kind of *bête noire*, the universal cause of human misery. For example, Dr Greville, an ideal Anglican clergyman in Richard Graves's satiric novel *The Spiritual Quixote*, affirmed: '... as a true rational system of religion contributes to the happiness of society, and of every individual; so enthusiasm not only tends to the confusion of society, but to undermine the foundation of all religion, and to introduce, in the end, scepticism of opinion, and licentiousness of practice.'

Despite this gloomy depiction of the effects of enthusiasm some writers, evangelical and non-evangelical, recognized that the term was being carelessly used, that it was often only a convenient weapon with which to flail an opponent. The same Dr Greville, who had depicted the chaos resulting from enthusiasm, warned his misled parishioner, Geoffrey Wildgoose, against Laodicism: 'Not that I wish to see you less serious in the practice of religion, nor even less an enthusiast, in some sense; as I am convinced nothing great can be effected without some degree of enthusiasm....' This ideal priest is obviously not using the term in a completely derogatory sense. But by far the most unequivocal, though negative, defence of the term came from John Wesley himself, who was as frightened of the baleful plague enthusiasm as most of the rest of the eighteenth century. To a young man who had asked whether George Whitefield's journals were not 'd—d cant, enthusiasm from end to end', Wesley replied: 'Whatever is spoke of the religion of the heart, and of the inward workings of the Spirit of God, must appear enthusiasm to those who have not felt them; that is, if they take upon them to judge of the things which they own they know not.'[4]

It is clear, however, that although not everyone in the century

[4] *The Journal of the Rev. John Wesley, A.M.*, ed. Nehemiah Curnock, 8 vols. (Standard Edn, London, 1938), II.319. Since references to the *Journal* are to this edition, hereafter I shall simply give the date of the entry.

accepted the basic definition of enthusiasm as a false belief in inspiration by the Holy Spirit, the connotations of the term were rarely favourable. Those individuals most likely to be called enthusiasts, those asserting that the Holy Spirit could and did speak to men even in enlightened England, generally used the term with fewer unfavourable connotations.

Yet some anti-enthusiastic writers accepted the basic definition as a false belief in inspiration, elaborated upon it, and drew conclusions from it. If the inspiration which the Methodists alleged to receive did not come from God, it must come from Satan. John Kirkby, rector of Blackmanstone in Kent, asserted in 1750 in *The Imposter Detected* that Methodism '... advances the same wicked Spirit [Satan] into the Place of God himself, making his diabolical Illusions and Suggestions pass for the Operations of the Holy Ghost'. Others, like the anonymous author of an application of a new edition of *A Fine Picture of Enthusiasm* (1744) to the Methodists, saw Christianity under the hands of the Methodists becoming 'a *passionate, mechanical* Religion', almost like Swift's delineation of the mechanical operations of the Spirit. The anti-enthusiast saw too that the enthusiast—and he accepted the premise that the Methodist was one—was making each individual his own religious authority. Obviously, the enthusiast, receiving what he believed were instructions straight from God, was unwilling to pay much respect to the other two sources of Christian dogma, the Scriptures and the Church. The true enthusiast particularly would not acknowledge the supremacy of the Scriptures if they conflicted with his private directions.[5] Even John Wesley acknowledged this as a characteristic of the enthusiast, although not of the Methodist, when in his *Journal* for 17th January 1739 he described '... two persons, who, I doubt are properly enthusiasts. For, first, they think to attain the end without the means, which is enthusiasm, properly so called. Again they think

[5] Umphrey Lee, *The Historical Backgrounds of Early Methodist Enthusiasm*, p. 62.

themselves inspired by God, and are not. But false, imaginary inspiration is enthusiasm. That theirs is only imaginary inspiration appears hence, *It contradicts the law and the testimony.*'[6] An almost inevitable result of such a belief was religious anarchy.

Finally the enthusiast was considered to be either hypocritical or insane. By alleging that God spoke directly to him, he was flying in the face of 'the *Law* of *Nature*, and right reason'. Nature and nature's laws revealed the clarity and the order of the world and ultimately of God. Reason was the means by which the individual believer, examining the truth of Christianity as he would examine that of any other theory, determined its validity. Locke had written: 'If he [God] would have us assent to the truth of any proposition, he either evidences that truth by the usual methods of natural reason, or else makes it known to be a truth which he would have us assent to by his authority, and convinces us that it is from him, by some marks which reason cannot be mistaken in. Reason must be our last judge and guide in everything.' The individual who deliberately affirmed a non-rational basis for his belief, who alleged that he was inspired by God, either was hypocritical in alleging what was obviously false or was deluded. The identification of enthusiasm with insanity was supported, in Umphrey Lee's words, by '... the physical phenomena often attending the "visitation of the Spirit" '[7]— the sudden fallings to the ground and the uttering of what was apparently gibberish—but the eighteenth-century attitude toward enthusiasm was based principally upon the opinions the enthusiast espoused. The possible conclusions which one might draw are unequivocally stated by an anonymous anti-Methodist: 'If they [the Methodist leaders] really believe what they have declared to the world, they must be the *maddest of all enthusiasts.* I leave it to you [the correspondent] to characterize your friends.'[8]

---

[6] The italics are mine.
[7] *The Historical Backgrounds of Early Methodist Enthusiasm*, p. 99.
[8] *A Letter to the Rev. Mr M--re B-k-r, Concerning the Methodists* (Dublin, 1752), p. 27.

Although the Methodists themselves defended inspiration on the basis of the Scriptures and asserted that the Holy Spirit, which had visited the Apostles and the primitive Church, could and also did visit eighteenth-century Methodists, the conventional Anglican and conservative reply as expressed by John Green, Bishop of Lincoln, was that the extraordinary powers then granted by God were necessary for the early church but '... were neither promised, nor seem necessary, nor appear to have been granted in following ages'.[9] To the anti-Methodist the Methodist claim to inspiration was clearly invalid: he had no proof. The Methodist asserted that he was inspired, but his critic, following in the track delineated by Locke, saw that the Methodist was totally unable to verify his claim. The anti-Methodist critic examined Methodism as earlier Locke had examined Christianity. The apostles, after Pentecost, had been given thaumaturgical powers. Their allegation of inspiration was verifiable by evidence, the miracles they worked. The Methodist had no such powers and worked no miracles. One anti-Methodist, replying to an answer to Dr Joseph Trapp, who had warned in 1739 against excessive righteousness, attacks the Methodist author's avowal of Whitefield's inspiration: 'It is contrary to my Apprehension, that this Holy Spirit should single out a Particular from amidst Numbers, enable and endue him with the largest Portions of his Grace to perform and forward the Work of the Ministry, and yet leave him without any other Proof than his own bare Word for it.'[10]

The eighteenth-century's charge of enthusiasm against the Methodists rested, then, upon what it assumed to be a false belief in the inspiration of the Holy Spirit. Although, as Umphrey Lee suggests, the individual Methodist's enthusiasm might carry him only to an awareness of a personal relationship with God and to a change of his life in conformity to the demands of

[9] *The Principles and Practices of the Methodists Considered* (London, 1761), pp. 4–5.
[10] *Observations and Remarks on Mr Seagrave's Conduct and Writings* (London, 1739), p. 4.

that relationship,[11] the conservative anti-Methodist saw a presumptuous attempt to ignore the commands of God as laid down in His Scriptures, as developed by tradition in the Church, and as revealed in the natural order of the world. In the simplest terms, the enthusiast was a knave or a madman.

The attack on Methodist enthusiasm was most pointed in the satires. The satire is roughly parallel to the attitudes and conclusions of the non-satiric anti-Methodist tracts, although in some cases the satirists pressed the conclusions farther. They attack the Methodist claim to inspiration by asserting that it derives from hypocrisy or madness, taunt the Methodist with an inability to prove that inspiration, ridicule the Methodist attribution of everyday occurrences to divine intervention, and bitterly castigate what they consider a denial of reason and a deification of the irrational.

The Methodist pretension to inspiration, to intimate acquaintance with God, was regularly attributed to madness or knavery. The ignorant but good-hearted Methodist servant, Humphry Clinker, in Smollett's novel, after being reproved for preaching, explains that he had 'an inward Admonition of the spirit'. Bramble, his employer, replies: 'You are either an hypocritical knave, or a wrong-headed enthusiast. . . . If you are a quack in sanctity and devotion, you will find it an easy matter to impose upon silly women, and others of crazed understanding, who will contribute lavishly to your support. If you are really seduced by the reveries of a disturbed imagination, the sooner you lose your senses entirely, the better for yourself and the community. . . . If you have just reflection enough left to maintain the character of a chosen vessel in the meetings of the godly, you and your hearers will be misled by a Will-o'-the-wisp, from one error into another, till you are plunged into religious frenzy. . . .'[12] Simple madness here is the least objectionable of the fates awaiting the enthusiast. That the inspiration was really

[11] *The Historical Backgrounds of Early Methodist Enthusiasm*, p. 146.
[12] *The Works of Tobias Smollett*, intro. W. E. Henley, 12 vols. (New York, 1899), III.225–6.

delusion is implied by the dramatist Samuel Foote, who, in an attempt to render invalid a Methodist defence that Socrates also believed in inspiration, asserted that Socrates and the Methodists were under the influence of a spirit, an evil one:

In short then, Sir, . . . *Socrates*, the Divine *Socrates*, was to all Intents and Purposes, an absolute Methodist, fatally for himself, a deluded frantic Methodist.

Strange as this Assertion may appear, to the Principles of what other Sect can we apply his repeated Declaration, of being under the immediate Influence of a Demon or Familiar, that he had a Voice within him that urged him to an Action, or restrained him from it. . . .[13]

Other satirists attributed the alleged inspiration to laziness. For example, Nathaniel Snip, a fictional lay preacher, grows weary of work, and the satirist comments in his own person: 'The usual Motive to Inspiration among our modern Lay-Teachers.'[14]

The failure of the Methodist to prove his inspiration was depicted ironically by the author of *A Plain and Easy Road to the Land of Bliss* (1761), a continuation of the allegory of the coats of Swift's *A Tale of a Tub*, who makes his Methodist apologist admit that the inspiration cannot be demonstrated. The apologist, unable to support his assertions, claims that his leader will provide proof: 'If anyone doubts of the truth of what I have affirm'd, let him come to Mr —— [a Methodist leader, probably Whitefield], and *he* will furnish him with proof sufficient, from his own dreams, visions, fancies, reveries, and revelations.' The apologist is unconsciously ironic. For the anti-Methodist nothing was more obvious than that the Methodist was a false prophet; he could not demonstrate his inspiration by visible or logical proof.

One of the things about the Methodist which most infuriated the anti-Methodist was his attribution of natural events to

[13] *A Letter from Mr Foote, to the Reverend Author of the Remarks, Critical and Christian on The Minor* (London, 1760), pp. 11–12.
[14] *A Journal of the Travels of Nathaniel Snip, a Methodist Teacher of the Word* (London, 1761), p. [7].

supernatural causes. Such irrational and enthusiastic behaviour was naturally singled out for satire. That John Wesley himself was prone to such supernatural explanations is well known. For example, in his *Journal* for 20th June 1774 Wesley records what was almost a fatal accident involving runaway horses. After a recital of the events he wrote: 'I am persuaded both evil and good angels had a large share in this transaction; how large we do not know now, but we shall know hereafter.' On the other hand, many of the Wesleyan explanations of divine intervention, and those of other Methodists as well, were the kind of attributions that Christians of all times have made. Early in his career, 24th September 1739, Wesley wrote: 'In my return [from Plaistow], a person galloping swiftly rode full against me, and overthrew both man and horse, but without any hurt to either. Glory be to Him who saves both man and beast.' Yet to many anti-Methodists this praise of God because injury had been avoided was sheer superstition. Wesley presumably would not have glorified God less even if man and horse had been hurt. But the praise of God implied that He had intervened to save His servant from injury. Thus the author of *The Principles and Practices of the Methodists Considered* in 1761 expressed in non-satiric terms his resentment at the Methodist practice: 'What ever business they [the Methodist leaders] are engaged in, though sometimes of no mighty importance, whatever errand they go about, though often not of the greatest significancy, it is still the *Lord's doing*. Whether they are at home or abroad, in good or evil plight, whether it rains or clears up, whether they escape a shower or are wetted by it, it is all owing to some divine direction, and made to answer some great purpose.'

The satire of this Methodist practice was almost parallel to this non-satiric statement. Samuel Foote, in a *Letter from Mr Foote* in 1760, wrote of George Whitefield: 'If he is bit by Fleas, he is buffetted by *Satan*. If he has the good Fortune to catch them, God will subdue his Enemies under his Feet....' James Lackington, the literary bookseller, indicated in his memoirs the extent to which this habit had gone: 'And I remember to have seen on a board, near Bed-minister-down, "Tripe and Corn-heels sold here as usual, except on the Lord's day which the *Lord help me to keep.*" ... I also saw in a village near Plymouth in Devonshire, "Roger Tuttell, *by God's grace and mercy*, kills rats, moles, and all sorts of vermin and venomous creatures".' In the *Journal of the Travels of Nathaniel Snip* the satire of the practice of attributing natural events to supernatural causes more obviously implies divine intervention. Snip, a tailor who has entered upon a career of preaching because he is tired of working, is unsuccessful in his first attempts at field oratory. When he speaks, he is reviled by the crowd. He records the subsequent events in his *Journal*: 'But as their Malice increased it pleased the Lord to pour upon their unbelieving Heads a most violent Shower of Rain, which scattered my Foes from about me, as Wind doth the Chaff when winnowed from the Corn of the Field....' As he continued his journey, he was able to report an obvious example of God's favour. It began to rain violently: 'On this I began an Hymn of Thanksgiving when (Oh ye Unbelievers behold the Hand of Heaven in this) scarce had I ended one Stave, when the Wind ceased, and the Storm was hushed.—*Great and marvellous are thy Doings, O Lord.*'

Finally the anti-Methodist attacked what he considered a denigration of reason and an extolling of fancy. In his eyes the Methodist asserted that the will of God as expressed through the operations of the Holy Spirit, or what the Methodist alleged to be that will, was obviously superior to simple reason or common sense. The Methodist affirmed the superiority of his private sense to the common sense, that knowledge common to all rational men. And in George Sherburn's words, 'To prefer one's "private" sense to common sense is irrational enthusiasm'.[15] The superiority of inspiration to reason is indicated satirically by the author of *A Plain and Easy Road to the Land of Bliss*, whose

[15] *A Literary History of England*, ed. Albert C. Baugh (New York, 1948), p. 827.

Methodist spokesman attacks the Martinists'—i.e. the Anglican—reliance on reason: 'They [the Martinists] make use of their reason to explain things, which is the sure way to be deceived;—whereas we go by nothing but puffs, dreams, visions, reveries, voices, &c. &c., all which are the truth itself.' Satirically the private vision is truth; the knowledge attained by logical and rational means is likely to be false. Earlier this spokesman, refuting a Martinist charge, had denied the validity of reason: '. . . I don't believe a single word of it; and, if any body asks my reason for it, I neither can nor will give any; for, at our orator's request, we have done with that foolish thing, call'd *reason*, long ago.' Satirically he has abandoned all logic, all common sense.

The Methodist denigration of reason was believed to be deliberate. But to the anti-Methodist it was obvious that the Methodist denied the authority of reason because he knew that his position was unreasonable. But by denying the supremacy of reason, he left himself open to the caprices of fancy, which could culminate only in madness. Thus the anti-Methodist satirist makes the Methodist follow his path to the logical end: the Methodist deliberately extols insanity. Nathaniel Lancaster, burlesquing the epic conventions, in his mock epic *Methodism Triumphant* (1767) invokes divine Mania:

> Oh! how unequal to the arduous height
> Of this great theme, without thy mighty aid,
> O thou celestial Source of Ecstacies,
> Of Visions, Raptures, and converting Dreams.
> Awful Ebriety of New-Birth Grace!
> Thee, MANIA, I invoke my pen to guide,
> To fire my soul, and urge my bold career.

His hero, modelled upon John Wesley, at the close of a sermon calls, 'O MANIA! O PHANTASIA! Pow'rs Divine!' to complete the work of regeneration. Other satirists were content to depict reason itself, the richest gift that God had given to man, corrupted.[16]

As seen by its opponents, religious enthusiasm thus culminated in its inevitable result, insanity. Against the menace of enthusiasm, which substituted the individual whim for the common aim, which threatened to return an enlightened nation to the bonds of superstition, and which promised fair to fill the mad houses to overflowing, the anti-Methodist fought with every weapon he had. Not the least of these was ridicule.

---

[16] See [Evan Lloyd,] *The Methodist, a Poem* (London, 1766), p. 12.

CHAPTER THREE

Satire of Methodist Doctrines

SINCE RELIGIOUS enthusiasm in the eighteenth century was more a matter of doctrine than of the manner in which the doctrine was presented—i.e. *what* was preached rather than *how* it was preached—a consideration of the satiric reaction to Methodist doctrine is a logical next step. We need to recognize at the beginning three equally important but conflicting facts: first, religious historians, with some disagreement, have seen little basic difference between the doctrine of the Wesleyan Methodists and that of the Church of England; secondly, the eighteenth-century Methodists asserted that there was no doctrinal difference; and, thirdly, the anti-Methodist was convinced that Methodism was subverting not only the doctrine of the Church of England but of all Christianity as well and that Methodist doctrine was sheer antinomianism. A brief examination of these generalizations will provide a background for approaching the satire of doctrine.

Writers on Wesleyan Methodism are generally agreed that the Methodists were attempting no innovations in doctrine. Although his anti-Methodist bias is evident, Lecky, the historian of the eighteenth century, admits this: 'It is ... certain that they [Wesley and Whitefield] held the doctrines of the Articles and the Homilies with an earnestness very rare among their brother clergymen, that none of their peculiar doctrines were in conflict with those doctrines, and that Wesley at least was attached with an even superstitious reverence to ecclesiastical forms.'[1] A later historian provides a clearer explanation of the

[1] *A History of England in the Eighteenth Century*, p. 51. It is possible that the very earnestness with which the Methodists held the doctrines of the Thirty-nine Articles could have won them many enemies, since the Calvinist

Methodist contribution to religious doctrine: 'Its [Methodism's] doctrines remained those of the Church of England, although by new emphasis it gave them fresh life, and certain dogmas, as those of Justification by Faith and Christian Perfection, it brought into prominence.'[2] Other writers suggest that Christian perfection was the only distinct Methodist doctrinal addition.[3] This doctrine then is the one exception to an identification of Methodist with Anglican doctrine. Christian perfection and the re-emphasized justification by faith were most seized upon as the subject of satire.

The semi-official Methodist attitude is clear. Wesley himself, who spoke for all Wesleyan Methodists, claimed that there was no doctrinal difference between the Methodists and the Church of England. He records in his *Journal* for 13th September 1739:

A serious clergyman desired to know in what points we differed from the Church of England. I answered, 'To the best of my knowledge, in none. The doctrines we preach are the doctrines of the Church of England; indeed the fundamental doctrines of the Church, clearly laid down, both in her Prayers, Articles, and Homilies.'

He asked, 'In what points, then, do you differ from the other

Methodists, particularly, were fond of quoting the Articles to opponents to demonstrate that they were wrong. The Articles themselves were in a certain disrepute. Although all university students as prospective clergy had to sign the Articles (Lecky, p. 27), according to Elliott-Binns (*The Early Evangelicals: A Religious and Social Study*, p. 171) an attempt, known as the Feathers' Tavern Case, was made 'to persuade Parliament to abolish subscription to the Articles'. The editor of *A Fine Picture of Enthusiasm* (London, 1744), p. 26, actually praised the Anglican clergy for not teaching the Articles. The conventional reply to the Calvinists that the Articles were articles of compromise was bitterly attacked by Richard Hill, in *Pietas Oxoniensis: or, A Full and Impartial Account of the Expulsion of Six Students from St Edmund Hall, Oxford* (London, 1768), who wrote: 'But for the sake of filthy lucre, to carry on a solemn farce of subscribing to Articles, which many of the subscribers no more believe, than they do Mother Goose's Tales, and then to form excuses for this horrid mockery, by calling them Articles of *Peace* instead of Articles of *Faith*, is such a degree of impious jesuitical equivocation, as without speedy repentance must draw down the just vengeance of a long-suffering GOD upon our land' (p. 74).

[2] Frederick C. Gill, *The Romantic Movement and Methodism* (London, 1937), p. 23.
[3] See particularly Richard M. Cameron, *The Rise of Methodism: A Sourcebook* (New York, 1954), p. 227.

clergy of the Church of England?' I answered, 'In none from that part of the clergy who adhere to the doctrines of the Church; but from that part of the clergy who dissent from the Church (though they own it not), I differ in the points following. . . .'

Although in 'the points following' Wesley gave a detailed list of his differences with some of the clergy on the meanings principally of justification, sanctification, and the new birth, he asserted that Methodist doctrine was Anglican doctrine.

The position of the anti-Methodist and the vehemency of that position are made clear by a passage from a warning to the clergy, *Methodism Examined and Displayed* (1759), by John Downes, rector of St Michael's, Wood Street: 'I have shewed you that their [the Methodists'] Doctrines or Notions square or coincide with many of the oldest and rankest Heresies that ever defiled the Purity, and disturbed the Peace of the Christian Church from its first Institution. . . .' On one hand the Methodist staunchly asserted his belief in what he called Church of England doctrine; on the other the anti-Methodist inveighed against a revival of heresy. The positions of the Methodist and the anti-Methodist were completely opposed.

Although certain doctrines such as justification by faith and Christian perfection were singled out for special abuse and satire, satiric attacks were made upon almost every possible point of doctrine. The Methodist justification by faith and the resulting denial of the efficacy of good works were bitterly satirized; yet at the height of the Calvinist-Wesleyan controversy in the seventies the strength of the Wesleyan opposition to what it considered antinomianism resulted in almost equally bitter satire of Methodist Arminianism and what the satirist called 'salvation by works'. Strangely, the satirists even attacked the Methodists for not having any doctrine. The satiric attack on Methodist doctrines, some of course genuinely Methodist and some only supposedly so, concentrated on the following: the doctrine of justification by faith and inefficacy of and lack of necessity for good works; the doctrine of assurance; the concept of the absence of sin in the elect; the doctrine of perfection; Arminianism and salvation by works; and the absence of any doctrine.

The doctrine of justification by faith is overtly stated in the Articles of Religion. Article XI reads: 'We are accounted righteous before God, only for the merit of our Lord and Saviour Jesus Christ by Faith, and not for our own works or deservings. Wherefore, that we are justified by Faith only, is a most wholesome Doctrine, and very full of comfort, as more largely is expressed in the Homily of Justification.'[4] Some anti-Methodists, as we have seen, objected to the Articles of Religion themselves, and some Methodists, like the Reverend Mr Richard Hill, a Calvinist, accused the Anglican authorities of ignoring the Articles for which English Protestants had been martyred. But most of the doctrinal controversy centred not upon the validity of the doctrine but upon the Methodist interpretation of justification by faith.

Obviously for the Anglican there was no *ex cathedra* definition of the article. His attitude varied from the mild statement of the author of the *Earnest and Affectionate Address to the People Called Methodists* (1745) to that of John Downes. The former wrote in defence of the Anglican clergy: 'Our Clergy neither deny *Justification by Faith*, in the true and just sense, nor have been wanting in inculcating it. They have been indeed very frequently charged with departing from the Doctrines of the Reformation, and with contradicting the Articles of our Church, on this Head. But there is not the least Foundation for such a Charge.' In attempting to 'justify' the necessity of good works, a minor problem faced by holders of the doctrine, he wrote: 'The Necessity of them [good works] in every one, who

[4] For reason of simplicity I am using the term *justification by faith* to refer to the whole concept of salvation by faith, although the two are not precisely synonymous, at least in a Methodist sense. The Methodists distinguished between justification and sanctification, the latter being an advanced condition of holiness. Yet presumably sanctification by faith was a part of salvation by faith. See *Encyclopaedia of Religion and Ethics* (1951), XI.183.

is justified or received to God's Favour, is all along supposed and insisted on, notwithstanding they cannot of themselves give us any claim to Mercy. . . .' On the other hand, the Reverend Mr Downes, who represents a kind of conservative extreme, asserted: 'The Methodists consider Man as a mere Machine, and as such unable to do anything for himself, or toward his own Salvation. . . .'

This Anglican priest saw the Methodist justification by faith not as a triumphant affirmation of Christ's sacrifice but as a denial of responsibility. Between these two extremes and thus perhaps more representative of the Anglican position is a statement attributed to a Richard Hardy, perhaps vicar of Knoulton in Nottinghamshire: 'Methodists (at least their Lay-Preachers) teach, that *Christians* are under no *obligation* to observe the *ten* Commandments; that Christ has done *all* for us, and that we need, therefore, do nothing for *Ourselves*.'[5]

A Methodist explanation of the term may provide a clearer basis for understanding the satires. John Wesley, in his famous 'Salvation by Faith' sermon, asserted that the individual could deserve nothing at God's hand. He then affirmed through a series of rhetorical questions that even a man's holy works could not atone for any of his sins. Nevertheless in the same sermon Wesley emphasized that faith is '. . . necessarily productive of all good works, and all holiness'. A more characteristic statement of the doctrine comes in the description of his own conversion by John Berridge, vicar of Everton and later a prominent Methodist. It is characteristic particularly in the extravagance of the language. Berridge wrote that he had become convinced of his own lack of faith and asked God for help: 'As I was sitting in my House one Morning, and musing upon a Text of Scripture, the following Words were darted into my Mind with

---

[5] [Richard Hardy] *A Letter from a Clergyman to One of His Parishioners, Who Was Inclined to Turn Methodist* (London, 1753), pp. 23–4. My identification of Hardy is tentative. Of the three Richard Hardys who attended Cambridge during the first half of the century, this one seems the likeliest candidate.

THE
SAINTS.
A
SATIRE.

———" Hypocrify, *and* Nonfenfe,
" *Have got th'*Advowfon *of their* Confcience."

HUDIBRAS.

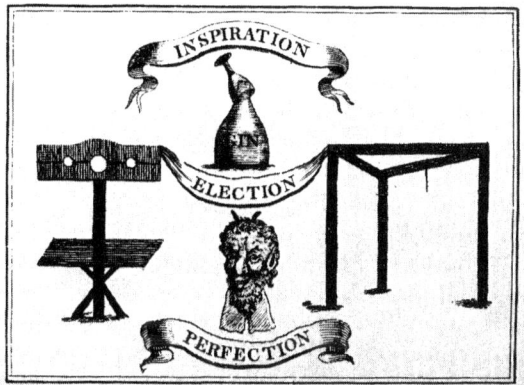

I cannot fee with Temper fo many religious Mountebanks impofe on the unwary Multitude; Wretches who make a Trade of Religion, and fhew an uncommon Concern for the next World only to raife their Fortunes with greater Security in this.   HYPOCRITE, Act I. Scene I.

LONDON,
Printed for J. BEW, in Pater-Nofter-Row.
MDCCLXXVIII.

The Saints was later entitled *The Fanatic Saints*. The author was one of the bitterest attackers of Methodism. In his 'advertisement' of *Sketches for Tabernacle-Frames* he wrote: '. . . *this Tribe* of *Mock-Saints* (but especially their *Leaders*) wrest and torture *Scripture* to their own *worldly Purposes*, and substitute various *false Doctrines* (favourable to their own *Designs*) instead of *moral Honesty, Integrity, Truth*, and the plain and clear Import of the holy Scriptures. Such *pious Imposters* the *Author* treats as *lawful Game*.'

wonderful Power, and seemed indeed like a Voice from Heaven (viz) "*Cease from thy own Works. . .*". Before I heard these Words, my Mind was in a very unusual Calm; but as soon as I heard them, my Soul was in a Tempest directly, and the Tears flowed from my Eyes like a Torrent.'[6] He continued: 'The Truth is, though I saw myself to be a Sinner, and a great Sinner, yet I did not see myself an utter lost Sinner, and therefore I could not come to Jesus Christ alone to save me; despised the Doctrine of Justification by Faith alone, looking on it as a foolish and a dangerous Doctrine; I was not yet stript of all my Righteousness, could not consider it all as filthy Rags. . . .' The anti-Methodist apparently paid less attention to Wesley's insistence upon good works than to accounts like Berridge's, which emphasized the filthy rags of one's own righteousness. To the anti-Methodist such scorn for righteousness was an invitation to antinomianism.

There is little direct satire of the positive side of the doctrine of justification by faith. Few of the orthodox were willing to ridicule the assumption that they were saved by Christ's merits rather than their own, but the satirists were quick to seize upon the scorn for righteousness, the denigration of good works, expressed by many Methodists. For the satirists not only did the doctrine prepare the way for antinomianism but it also challenged their basic philosophic assumptions. The idea that one could perform a righteous or a moral act only after he had become aware of the saving grace of God was opposed by the eighteenth-century conception of morality as a necessary subordination of an individual's desires and tastes to the good of society. The contempt for the value of conventional morality once again asserted, as the anti-Methodist believed Methodist enthusiasm had, the superiority of the individual's desires and whims over those of the society. In other words, it destroyed the basis of an empirical morality.

[6] [John Berridge] *Justification by Faith Alone* (2nd edn, London [1758]), p. 13.

Secondly the assertion that good works could not precede an emotional act of belief would have seriously conflicted with the idea of an ordered, rational world. It would make all virtue, all goodness, depend upon the irrational whim of an irrational Deity. Such a doctrine would unmake the creation, would turn the ordered universe of the eighteenth century back to chaos.

Thus, the satire of the doctrine of justification by faith is almost always coupled with much severer satire of the denigration of good works. The anti-Methodist satirist, empiricist that he is, is primarily concerned not with the orthodoxy of the doctrine but with its practical results and its challenge to his world. Nevertheless in at least two works satire simply of the doctrine appears. Mr Williams, Shamela's clerical friend in Fielding's novel, preaches, according to Shamela: 'That 'tis not what we do, but what we believe, that must save us. . . .'[7] One may practice whatever he wishes so long as he believes. Jemina Cawdle, a minor character representing Calvinistic Methodism in Richard Cumberland's *Henry* (1795), says: 'Let us have faith and grace, and it matters little what we do, or what we omit to do.'

The most elaborate satire of justification by faith and the inefficacy of and lack of necessity for good works appears in *A Plain and Easy Road to the Land of Bliss*. The work uses as its principal device the coat, allegorically religious faith, drawn from Jonathan Swift's *A Tale of a Tub*. Here the coat has a seam running through the middle of the upper part. On the right side of the coat is stitched *belief*, on the left *performance*. The author then describes the Methodist actions; their similarity to Jack's [the dissenter's] in the original satire is obvious: 'What does this adventurer [the Eolist, or Methodist] then do?—He took an old snipp'd pen-knife, and cut, or rather haggled, his coat down the back, from top to bottom; yet not so even but there remained—upon the left side—some jaggs and tatters, occasioned

---

[7] Henry Fielding, *An Apology for the Life of Mrs Shamela Andrews*, ed. Sheridan W. Baker, Jr. (Berkeley and Los Angeles, 1953), p. 40.

by the badness of his tool.—These he call'd filthy rags, and said that, according to one father *Paul's* interpretation of the will, they were sufficient for any man to wear upon the left side.' The satirist continues: 'In this fashion he enjoin'd his followers, for ever, to wear their coats; and threaten'd them, that if at any time they suffer'd any taylor (master or man) to make 'em another side to their coats, that they should all as surely be d—'d as ever they were born.' But the satire becomes more vigorous: '—and as he never mention'd the left side of the coat but with a full intention to run it down, (calling it, by the name of his own blunt penknife's making, filthy rags) by such means he is become the darling of all whoremongers, highwaymen, pickpockets, ladies of pleasure, bawds, drunkards, dishonest tradesmen, &c.—Finally, he takes in all sorts and sizes of your —*no-doers* and *wrong-doers.*'

The basic image of the filthy rags of righteousness is used effectively by Nathaniel Snip, the tailor turned lay-preacher, who preaches on the ineffectiveness of good works in a metaphor drawn from his trade but highly appropriate for the satirist's purpose: 'Good works is but a tatterred Garment: 'Tis, in Truth, a Pair of Breeches, a tatterred Pair of Breeches, without Linings, and I may say, that betrayeth our nakedness, and exposeth us to the Storms of Iniquity and the cloven Foot of our Grand Enemy.'[8] Other Methodist lay-preachers in the satires, like Geoffrey Wildgoose in *The Spiritual Quixote*, spoke metaphorically of the filthy rags of righteousness.

Other satiric references to the doctrine are frequent. Winifred Jenkins, the delightful illiterate of *Humphry Clinker*, who in the course of her master's travels for his health has been permitted to visit the Tabernacle, Whitefield's London chapel, sends her Mrs Mary Jones 'a sarment upon the nothingness of good works, which was preached in the Tabernacle. . . .'[9] Richard Graves wrote in *The Spiritual Quixote* that no matter what text

---

[8] *Journal of the Travels of Nathaniel Snip*, pp. 17-18.
[9] Smollett, *Works*, I.253.

Whitefield preached upon, he always ended with: 'Down with your good works!' Continuing his attack, he wrote: 'Mr Whitfield . . . said little about repentance, but laid all the stress upon faith alone; so that if a man was, or fancied, or even said, that he was possessed of true faith, he was immediately pronounced a convert; and, whether he reformed his life or not, became a saint upon easy terms.'[10] The author of *A Letter of Expostulation from the Manager of the Theatre in Tottenham-Court, to the Manager of the Theatre in the Hay-Market*, one of the pamphlets resulting from Foote's *The Minor*, makes Dr Squintum, one of the satiric labels assigned to Whitefield, proclaim:

> Faith, like a whirlwind, shall waft us on wings,
> Good works are but paultry mechanical things. . . .

Urging Foote to join him in a lucrative profession, field preaching, Squintum says that there is no need for him to change his present way of life, that no reform is necessary.

The mildest satire of the doctrine comes in Lackington's *Memoirs*. Before Lackington's conversion, a Methodist assured him that morality was of no value, that good works were only 'splendid sins', that faith did everything, that faith came through justification, and that justification '. . . was a sudden operation on the soul, by which the most execrable wretch that ever lived might instantaneously be assured all his sins being pardon'd. . . .' After Lackington's conversion, whenever he had a chance to read aloud from the Bible at family prayers and the like, he chose '. . . such verses as I deemed favourable to the doctrine of Original Sin, Justification by Faith, imputed Righteousness, the doctrine of the Trinity, &c.'. Yet as often as Lackington read from St Paul's epistles on justification by faith, his mistress read from St James's on the value of good works. Lackington, feeling that he has more texts on his side, writes:

---

[10] Graves, II.8–9. Whitefield's name is spelled both with and without the medial *e*.

'As to St James, I was almost ready to conclude, that he was not quite orthodox, and so I did not much mind what he said.'

The falsity of belief in the doctrine of justification by faith and the denigration of good works was demonstrated in a device which is so often used in the satires that it is almost a convention. Probably originated by Samuel Foote in *The Minor*, the device centres on a carefully pious procuress who sees no conflict between her trade and her faith, Methodism. After Mrs Cole in *The Minor* has carelessly talked of regeneration, the new birth, and the like, she then solicits her customer. After Mrs Cole's departure, the customer draws the moral for the audience: 'How the jade has jumbled together the carnal and spiritual. With what ease she reconciles her new birth to her old calling.' *The Methodist, a Comedy*, (c. 1761), attributed to Israel Pottinger, a minor dramatist, called itself a continuation of *The Minor* and emphasized even more than *The Minor* had done the discrepancy between faith and works. Mrs Cole, still following her calling, says of another character and a fellow convert: 'Why, do you know that the Jade has been impudent enough to say that it was presumptuous to attend the Service of the Faithful while she followed a Course of Life so opposite to her Conscience—As if everybody ought not to labour in their Vocation, Mr *Squintum* [Whitefield]—Lord have mercy on me! what a wicked World we live in—.' Asked directly how she can reconcile keeping a house of prostitution with her religious scruples, she replies: 'Why, the Doctor [Squintum] knows that Works are of no Consequence toward a Future State, and that Faith is all.' *The Spiritual Minor*, using the same central characters, makes Mrs Cole slightly more squeamish. She says of the problem: 'The prejudice of education had filled me with fears of damnation, and I thought I could not carry on my business with a safe conscience; but he [Squintum] prov'd, by such cogent arguments, that we are to be sav'd by faith, and not by the works of the law, that I was convinced, and my conscience has ever since been at ease.' And Mr Rakish, one of Mrs Cole's customers, asserts pointedly: '. . . I'm something of a methodist myself: I have not the least apprehension of being damn'd, though I indulge myself in the full gratification of all my passions.' The device reappears in Graves's *The Spiritual Quixote* (1773). A Bristol brothel keeper comes to Geoffrey Wildgoose to get approval of her actions. Wildgoose tells her: 'Why, . . . without doubt, our outward actions are indifferent in themselves; and it is the heart that God chiefly regards. God *sees* no sin in the *elect*. If we have true faith, that will sanctify our works.' What the satirist considered Methodist antinomianism led directly to these results.

Probably the most devastating satire of justification by faith came in Smollett's *Launcelot Greaves* in 1751. Greaves, a Quixotic knight-reformer, is kidnapped and taken to a madhouse. He realizes where he is when he hears a voice denying the validity of good works. The identification of the insane speaker with a Methodist is made clear by the speech: 'Assuredly . . . he that thinks to be saved by works is in a state of utter reprobation—I myself was a profane weaver, and trusted to the rottenness of works— . . . but now I have got a glimpse of the new light—I feel the operations of grace—I am of the new birth—I abhor good works—I detest all working but the working of the spirit. . . .'[11] The conclusion implied by Smollett is that only a lunatic would disavow the usefulness of good works.

The next three doctrines which were attacked—assurance, the concept that the elect cannot sin, and perfection—although they are by no means synonymous, are closely related and, as the satires reveal, were frequently confused both by the non-theological and the theological mind. The first of these, assurance, meant for the Methodist an awareness that God had forgiven him his sins. That was the meaning John Wesley had in mind when he wrote in his *Journal* for 6th October 1738 apropos

[11] Smollett, *Works*, I.253.

of a sermon by the Reverend Mr Arthur Bedford, Chaplain to the Prince of Wales, attacking assurance: 'We speak of an assurance of our present pardon; not, as he does of our final perseverance.'[12] But that Methodist assurance was misunderstood as meaning assurance of salvation is clear by *The Question, Whether It Be Right to Turn Methodist* (1745). The anonymous author writes: '*Assurance*, is doubtless, a Christian Doctrine, and indeed one of the most comfortable Doctrines in Christianity: But they [the Methodists] do not consider there are *Two Kinds* of Assurance; and the Error lies in Confounding the one with the Other. One respects our Present State; the other refers to our *Future*. The first is the Assurance of *Faith*, by which we are, and ought to be assured, that we *are Christians*, and within the Covenant of Grace: The other is such an Assurance, as none can have but by Revelation, as *Daniel* and St *Paul*, and some other holy Persons have had, of the *Certainty of their Salvation*.' It was the assurance of salvation at which the satirists aimed their fire. Indeed the satiric attack on the doctrine in *The Fanatic Saints* in 1778 is almost parallel to the earlier non-satiric statement:

> *Christian-Assurance* in the *Gospel-Sense*
> They [the Methodists] construe into matchless
>   Impudence....

The second of these closely related ideas, the concept that the elect cannot sin, was obviously a wider target for the satirists and was more frequently satirized than the doctrine of assurance, despite the fact that it cannot be as closely identified with Methodism. John Wesley himself seems never to have made such an assertion. He comes closest in the expression of his views on 24th August 1743 as he prepared for a conference of the Wesleyan and Calvinistic Methodists and the Moravians, a

[12] *Journal*, II.83. Ronald Knox asserts that Whitefield, on the other hand, did regard the experience of the New Birth as giving the individual involved the conviction that he was 'irrevocably sealed for heaven'. (See p. 495.)

conference that was never held. There he did not deny that God had 'unconditionally elected some persons to eternal glory'. With regard to final perseverance—i.e. the ultimate salvation of such persons—he wrote that he was inclined to believe "That there is a state attainable in this life, from which a man cannot finally fall . . .'. Yet Wesley makes clear that such an elect are not the only ones who will attain salvation, and the view should be recognized as the extreme of the Wesleyan position written when he was attempting a reconciliation with the Calvinist Methodists.

The anti-Methodist position is stated effectively by Theophilus Evans, who presumably was a better historian than prophet: 'Though *Methodism* is now almost quite extinct, yet several of its dire Consequences still remain, as that Sin is no *Sin* in the Elect; that Faith can never be finally lost; and that *once* a Saint, *for ever* a Saint, as OLIVER said of himself. And consequently the most Zealous of the Party now in a great measure wallow in Lust and Sensuality, and never stick at anything, be it ever so heinous.'[13] In considering the doctrine, James Lackington is trenchant in his criticism. He writes: 'The pernicious consequences of such tenets [that the elect cannot sin] impressed on the minds of the ignorant followers of these quacks in religion, must be obvious to every person capable of reflection. They have nothing to do but to enlist themselves in the band of the Elect, and no matter then how criminal their life!' It is clear that the anti-Methodist feared antinomianism as a direct result of such a doctrine. This is the point which is laboured in the satire.

Jemina Cawdle, the notorious evil liver of Richard Cumberland's *Henry*, says that she cannot fall from grace, that she cannot be guilty. Samuel Bowden, writing in 1754, mocked in awkward quatrains:

[13] Theophilus Evans, *The History of Modern Enthusiasm, from the Reformation to the Present Times* (2nd edn, London, 1757), p. 1. The attempt to link Methodism with the earlier Puritan tradition has already been noted. See Chapter 1.

Here the knave, cheat, and liar, by grace are protected,
For the Lord sees no backsliding in his elected;
O! comforting creed! to sooth us in evil,
To rely all on faith—and to deal with the devil.[14]

The third of these doctrines, that of Christian perfection, is more clearly a Methodist one. It was generally viewed as a considerable step beyond justification. The *Encyclopaedia of Religion and Ethics* states that for Methodists:

... Christian perfection was the further seal of the Holy Spirit set upon the earnest striving of the regenerate will accompanied by a faith working by love; such faith made this blessing its direct object, received it as a gift of grace, and retained it by the obedience of faith which became fruitful and effective through an abiding union with the crucified and risen Redeemer. Indeed, the doctrine of a complete deliverance from all sin was regarded as the logical and experimental outcome of the proclamation of a free, full, present salvation as the gift of grace to every penitent sinner.

Yet the same definition recognizes that perfection did not free the individual from mistakes and that the attaining of it was a rare experience. Both Wesley and William Law, from whom Wesley derived his idea of perfection, agreed that perfection, once attained, might be lost.[15] Christian perfection, briefly, in the Methodist sense, is a state of holiness attained by only a few individuals in whom sin is unlikely to occur, but it is not an infallible state.

The satirists of the doctrine of perfection were quick to attribute to believers in it very imperfect behaviour. The author of *Perfection. A Poetical Epistle* (1778), largely an attack on Wesley, characterized an unidentified preacher in the following manner:

For *Sanctity*, and *Rapes on Babes*, well known;
Perfection's Child—a Suckling of *your* [Wesley's] *own*.
With *him Perfection's* Graft brought forth *good* Fruit,

[14] Samuel Bowden, *Poems on Various Subjects* (Bath, 1754), p. 214. The number of the stanza, 8, has been omitted.
[15] Eric W. Baker, *A Herald of the Evangelical Revival* (London, 1948), p. 79.

In *Faith* an Angel, and in *Works* a Brute: . . .
Thus thro' *Delusion's* Mist *Perfection* leads
God's chosen People to the worst of Deeds.

A Calvinist pamphlet, attributed to the Methodist Richard Hill, is as acidly satiric of the doctrine: 'Mr Wesley must also well remember a certain *perfect* married lady, who fancied that she was to be the mother of a great prophet, by means of a *perfect* preacher for whom she had conceived a *perfect* fondness; . . . it is certain a *perfect* child was born. . . .'[16] Other satirists alleged that the doctrine of perfection cloaked sexual immorality. The author of *The Fanatic Saints* (1778) even attributed such immorality to Wesley himself:

'Perfection only saves'—*John* gravely cries;
Mark how his *Life* his *Tenet* justifies!
'*The Husband of one Wife*' this Saint appears;
Who wou'd *suspect* his *Sanctity* and years?
. . . Whilst on the Sin of *Wantonness* he dwells,
His own weak Flesh at *sev'nty-five* rebels.

Although the Methodist insistence on justification by faith laid the movement open to charges of antinomianism, the insistence that all men could be saved (loosely Arminianism) and the closely allied insistence upon works brought the charges of Arminianism and of asserting salvation by works upon the heads of the Methodists. These charges came almost entirely from the Calvinist wing of Methodism itself. If all men could be saved, so the Calvinist Methodist reasoned, man could work for his own salvation and thus he would not be justified by faith alone. Yet it should be remembered, as T. W. Herbert emphasizes, that the Calvinist-Arminian controversy had been a continuing one within the Church of England and was an indication of the freedom allowed in theological belief.[17]

[16] [Richard Hill] *A Review of All the Doctrines Taught by the Rev. Mr John Wesley* (2nd edn, London, 1772), p. 49.
[17] *John Wesley as Editor and Author*, Princeton Studies in English, No. 17 (Princeton, 1940), p. 32.

SATIRE OF METHODIST DOCTRINES

The attacks on Arminianism and salvation by works erupted as a part of the bitter Calvinist controversy ushered in by the 1770 Methodist conference, at which it was agreed that the movement had leaned too much toward Calvinism.[18] Augustus M. Toplady, one of Wesley's bitterest foes, denounced him as 'a red-hot Arminian'.[19] Other Calvinists, like Richard Hill and Walter Shirley, accused the Wesleyans of maintaining salvation by works and urged them to recant the heresy and to return to Gospel truths. Rowland Hill, brother to Richard and one of the hottest of the red-hot Calvinists, provides a summary of the doctrinal basis of the attacks:

For this very same man [Wesley] that could so justly exclaim against himself in 1738, as the vilest of the vile, and against *seeking salvation by the works of the law*, can in 1770, solemnly declare before all his preachers, that we are *to do good works in order that we may find favour with God. That every believer works* FOR *as well as from life. That* ALL *who are convinced of sin* UNDERVALUE THEMSELVES *in* EVERY *respect; in short*, that we are to be rewarded ACCORDING TO THE MERIT OF WORKS.[20]

The clearest explanation of the Calvinist position comes in the pedestrian verse of Thomas Gurney, who asks:

> Shall *Wesley* sow his hurtful Tares,
> Or scatter around a thousand Snares;
> Telling how GOD from Wrath may turn,
> And love the Soul he thought to burn;
> And how, again his mind may move
> To hate, where he has vow'd to love;
> How all mankind he fain would save,
> Yet longs for what he cannot have. . . .[21]

---

[18] A detailed account of the controversy is given in Tyerman, *Life of John Wesley*, III.72–109. There is no evidence that Wesley and the Wesleyan Methodists put any more insistence on good works in 1770 than they had done earlier.

[19] *The Works of Augustus M. Toplady, A.B.* (new edn, London, 1825), V.317.

[20] Rowland Hill, *A Full Answer to the Rev. J. Wesley's Remarks upon a Late Pamphlet* (Bristol [1777]), p. 10 note. Rowland Hill had been the centre of a group of Methodists at Cambridge in 1764. See Barr, *Early Methodists Under Persecution*, p. 176.

[21] Thomas Gurney, *Poems on Various Occasions* (Sudbury, 1790), p. 3.

Clearly, however, the attacks were not so much upon the doctrine, since the Calvinists waste little time in refuting it, as upon the men who allegedly believed it.

In the same manner the satiric attacks on the doctrine are largely personal. The most effective of these, *The Foundry Budget Opened* (1780), by John MacGowan, a Calvinist Methodist who before his conversion had fought with the Pretender at Culloden, took the life of Wesley as a basis of attack on the doctrine: '. . . I shall set before you a summary view of *John's* works of merit. He hath not only repented and believed his own way, but he hath obeyed by fasting. *John* is given to fasting and mortification, therefore he is a rare example of devotion. In 1729, *John* began to mortify and to purify himself by fasting every Friday, so that now for the space of forty-two years, *John* hath fasted every Friday, and in this current year has not less than two thousand one hundred and eighty-four Fridays to place to his own credit with the Almighty.'

After a further enumeration of the hours Wesley has spent in preaching and praying, MacGowan then overtly links the doctrine of salvation by works and Wesley with Roman Catholicism:

Whether *John* fasted upon good fish on Friday, as his brethren on the Continent are said to do, or actually pinched his belly, I can not certainly tell, but surely no small dependence may be had upon *John's* works, if works are, as he tells us, the *condition of our salvation.* . . . But what a terrible thing would it be, if after all, *John* should lose all this perfection, and be damned at last? which very possibly may be the case according to his own doctrine.

This was how John Wesley worked his way toward heaven.

A small part of the satire of Methodist doctrine was aimed at the Methodist failure to enunciate its doctrine clearly. Some critics felt that Methodism had no essential doctrines and shifted its ground as the occasion demanded. Elliott-Binns, the historian of the evangelical movement, recognizing that the

SATIRE OF METHODIST DOCTRINES

Methodists largely accepted the doctrines of the Church, emphasizes that the doctrines were not insisted upon for membership in Methodist societies.[22] This is testified to by John Kirkby, who, writing in 1750, said that although the Methodist Church might not be holy, it was catholic since it was 'reconcileable to Persons of all Opinions'. One satirist, in *The Methodists*, attributed the absence of distinctive doctrine to Satanic inspiration. Satan, summarizing his past actions to undermine the Church of England and to strengthen Rome, explains his new strategy as he originates the Methodists:

... for your [Rome's] good,
I've form'd a new religious Brood,
Where all the various Sects in *One*,
In my *Alembick* mixt are thrown. ...

However, such satire forms an almost insignificant part of the whole satire of Methodist doctrine.

Thus, although the Methodists sought to avoid doctrinal innovations, the doctrines emphasized by them, particularly justification by faith and Christian perfection, were extensively satirized. The satirists, obviously enjoying the chance to smear the sanctimonious devotees of religion with the mud of immorality, generally depicted the Methodist believer as a notorious evil liver who used the doctrines as justification for the gratification of his own appetites. In the satires, justification by faith became justification for immorality; assurance and perfection became impudence and obvious corruption. Yet for many of the orthodox the antinomianism attributed to the Methodists in the satires was an only slightly exaggerated depiction of the results of belief in the Methodist doctrines.[23]

---

[22] *The Early Evangelicals: A Religious and Social Study*, p. 384.
[23] Although there are scattered attacks upon such things as the concept of lack of regeneration in the sacrament of baptism, they seem insignificant and do not form a clear pattern of attacks upon specific doctrines.

CHAPTER FOUR

Satire of Methodist Preachers and Preaching

ALTHOUGH THE anti-Methodists concentrated much of their fire upon the ideology of their enemy, they aimed a good many salvoes at Methodist actions which offended them. Many of these involved Methodist preachers and the way they preached. According to the satirists, the Methodist use of unordained preachers changed the ordered world of distinct divisions between the clergy and the layman into a world of confusion in which the priest and the layman could not be distinguished and in which the trades and the shops were empty because all were preaching God's word. These Methodist orators, as seen in the anti-Methodist publications, preaching in the fields, on the commons, and elsewhere, ranted, screamed, and used every possible rhetorical device to sway their audiences. They developed a peculiar vocabulary compounded of Scriptural phrases wrenched from their context and a nuptial language highly inappropriate to the occasion. The satire of Methodist preachers, Methodist preaching, and the vocabulary of Methodism reveals how deeply the eighteenth-century conservative was shocked by these elements of Methodism.

Both ordained and unordained preachers were attacked, but the lay preacher was singled out for extensive abuse. The use of lay preachers was not a phenomenon peculiar to eighteenth-century Methodism. But the use of them in the century particularly shocked the conservative, who were accustomed to a well-trained and largely even well-born clergy. The fastidious John Wesley was at first opposed to the practice. When a young Methodist layman, Thomas Maxfield, began preaching in London, Wesley's first impulse was to censure him for his irregular action, but when Wesley's mother warned him not to contradict what was apparently a call of God, Wesley desisted.[1] He soon accepted the fact that laymen as well as clergy could be called to preach, but the view of the orthodox clergyman did not change. That view was clearly stated.

Joseph Trapp, who had warned against excessive righteousness early in the progress of Methodism, objected even to the use of laymen for reading prayers: 'For *Laymen* to officiate in *reading Prayers* to any Assembly, except their *own Families*, is an Encroachment upon the Office of those who are ordain'd to holy Functions; and I fear takes off from the Reverence and Respect due to them. And for *unletter'd Laics* to take upon them to *expound* or *interpret* the Scriptures, is neither laudable, nor justifiable...' A less rigorous position is that of Edmund Gibson, Bishop of London. Fearing that the use of lay preachers would encourage completely unfit persons to choose preaching as a livelihood, he asked: 'Whether, if this *Itinerant* Way of Preaching may be taken-up by any one *at Pleasure*, without the least Enquiry as to *Abilities* or *Morals*, and without any *other Restraint* whatsoever; many Persons, who had no Provision or Settlement in Life, nor perhaps either Abilities or Morals, may not be tempted to put on the *Garb*, and to learn the genuine *Language* of a Methodist; as the best Expedient they can think of, to procure for themselves a comfortable Subsistence?'[2] Dr William Dodd objected to the use of unordained preachers on ecclesiastical and religious grounds. Referring to Wesley's disclaimer of any intention of separating from the Church, he wrote: '... I can not for my own Part conceive, what Sophistry of Argument can be sufficient to disprove *their* Separation, who have broke lose from all Obedience to their Ordinary; entirely leaped over all parochial Unity and Communion; ... who preach in all Places, without Reserve; And, (which is worst of all, and a Source, I am convinced by Experience, of innumerable

[1] Henry Carter, *The Methodist Heritage* (New York, 1951), p. 92.
[2] *Observations upon the Conduct and Behaviour of a Certain Sect Usually Distinguished by the Name of Methodists* (3rd edn, London, 1744), p. 24.

Evils,) who employ, and send forth Laymen of the most unlettered Sort, to preach the Gospel, without any Authority or Commission from God or Man.'

Some of the satirists, like their non-satiric counterparts, deplored the lack of ordination and dramatized the confusion which resulted. Samuel Foote, perennially antagonistic to Methodism, asserted half seriously in a letter to a clerical opponent: 'SIR, THOUGH no Man can have a higher Reverence for that Order amongst us, to which you lay Claim, than myself, yet the Jargon of the Tabernacle has so perverted the common Meaning of Words, that I am extremely puzzled in what Manner to address you; it being impossible to determine from the Title you assume, whether you are an Authoriz'd Pastor, or a Peruke-Maker; a real Clergyman, or a Corn-Cutter.'[3]

Generally, however, the satirists depicted the incongruity of laymen preaching and the practical results if everyone were to preach. One of the most effective attacks on Methodist lay preachers, Evan Lloyd's *The Methodist* (1766), explained their desire to preach to the presence of a Satanic spirit within them. The result of these blockheads, knaves, and dunces starting into preaching is vividly described. Lawyers throw aside Coke upon Littleton for the Bible:

> *Plaintiff, Defendant,* and *my Lord*
> Are banish'd, and now *Faith's* the Word. . . .

Physicians substitute the Prayer Book for Galen:

> *Salvation* now is All the *Cant*,
> *Salvation* is the *only* Want.
> . . . Of a *New-Birth* they prate, and prate
> While *Midwifry* is out of Date. . . .

It is a world in which none follows his proper trade. All men are intent on saving one another's souls:

[3] *A Letter from Mr Foote*, p. 1.

> The *Baker*, now a *Preacher* grown,
> Finds Man *lives not by Bread alone*. ...
> The *Brewer*, hit by Phrenzy's Grub,
> The *Mashing* for the *Preaching Tub*
> Resigns, *those Waters* to explore,
> Which if you drink, you *thirst no more*. ...

The same sort of world is depicted by the author of *The Fanatic Saints* (1778), although the inappropriateness of the actions of the new preachers is stressed:

> Today a *Link-Boy*, fir'd with *Inspiration*,
> *Trims up* and *lights* the *Lantern of Salvation:*
> Tomorrow *Strap*, who scorns to mend a *Shoe*,
> Sets *Gospel-Myst'ries* in the clearest View;
> Unfolds with Ease what *Christ* himself conceal'd,
> And proves that *all Things* are to *him* reveal'd.
> Brimful of *Righteousness*, unaw'd by *Sense*,
> By *Inspiration* urg'd and *Impudence*,
> The *Bricklayer's-Labourer*, with horny *Fists*,
> On *Faith* in Preference to Works insists.

Maw-worm, a lay preacher in Isaac Bickerstaff's *The Hypocrite*, leaves his shop to preach and later confesses: 'We have lost almost all our customers, because I keeps extorting them whenever they come into the shop.'[4] Perhaps because the cobbler permitted the satirist an easy pun on souls, the satirist often chose him as his subject. The man who should have cared for one kind of sole had the effrontery to try to care for another. Often too tailors were singled out, perhaps because of the appropriateness of the metaphor of 'filthy rags of righteousness'.

[4] Although the term *Methodist* is not used in Bickerstaff's play and although Bickerstaff wrote, 'Among the audiences of the present day the Cantwell [the hypocrite] of this piece will be variously attributed through the whole circle of fanatics, as one sect or another may from personal motives have become obnoxious to the spectator', it is clear that he has the Methodists in mind. *The Hypocrite, a Comedy Altered from C. Cibber* (London, 1792), p. Aiii^r.

Other satirists were content simply to characterize the new activities of the preachers in terms of their old trades. Thus, the fictional Nathaniel Snip, himself a lay preacher, records in his *Journal* that he heard in York '... the *Inspired Drummer* beat the *Tattoo* of Righteousness; the *Ravally*, as I may say, of Salvation. ...' A footnote by the anti-Methodist editor identified him as 'A Quixotish Wretch who fancies himself inspired; and who from being a common Drummer has taken up the safer and more profitable Employment of *Dry Nurse* to the *Newborn Babes of Grace* at the Tabernacle in York'. The author of a funeral discourse on the death of Laurence Sterne's Mr Yorick, perhaps Sterne himself, said of the deceased: '... it is well known, that YORICK was a preacher metamorphosed into a buffoon, and not a buffoon converted into a preacher.'[5] The implication is obvious.

In addition to being satirized for leaving his proper trade and assuming functions for which he had only the call of zeal,[6] the Methodist lay preacher was severely attacked for his presumption in preaching and in expounding the Scriptures when he himself was unlearned and perhaps even illiterate. While there is no indication that Wesley ever permitted such ignorant preachers of the gospel to practise under him, the nature of the religious revival, with relatively loose organizational control,

[5] *A Funeral Discourse Occasioned by the Much Lamented Death of Mr Yorick* (Aretopolis, 1761), p. 4.

[6] The Methodists were by no means silent in the face of these attacks. One of the most vigorous replies was one by the Calvinistic Methodist John MacGowan, who later lifted his cudgels against Wesley himself. MacGowan wrote concerning the expulsion of six students from St Edmund's Hall for irregular religious behaviour: 'It is thought that the Apostles would have been in much higher esteem with our dignified clergymen than they are, if their *birth and education had given them the rank of gentlemen*, and if they had not been *brought up in the lowest of trades* [a reference to the accusation that the expelled students had practiced trades] before conversion; especially if they had not contented themselves with being called by the plain names of Paul, Peter, &c., but had annexed D.D. or prefixed Rt Rev. to their proper names. And indeed it must be owned, that it would have been much more courtly and clerical in Paul to have begun his epistles thus: HIS GRACE, THE MOST REVEREND FATHER IN GOD PAUL LORD ARCHBISHOP OF ALL THE CHURCHES, *to the Saints and Faithful, &c., which are at, &c.*'

See *A Further Defence of Priestcraft; Being a Practical Improvement of the Shaver's Sermon on the Expulsion of Six Young Gentlemen from the University of Oxford, for Praying, Reading, and Expounding the Scriptures* (London, 1768), pp. 4–5.

made the appearance of such preachers likely. Wesley himself forced his unordained ministers to read and study six to eight hours per day.[7] They might be unordained, but they would be well grounded in theology and would have read some non-theological works carefully chosen by Wesley himself. Nevertheless the satire of Methodist lay preachers emphasized their ignorance and their complete lack of preparation for the function they espoused.

James Lackington asserted non-satirically that most Methodist preachers '. . . are very ignorant and extremely illiterate: many of these excellent spiritual guides cannot even read a chapter in the Bible, though containing the deep mysteries which they have the rashness and presumption to pretend to explain'. Of a particular preacher, once a mechanic, Lackington said: 'I am only sorry, as he lately was an honest useful tradesman, that he should have so much spiritual quixotism in him, as at thirty years of age to shut up his shop and turn preacher, without being able to read his primer. . . .' Lackington ironically asserted that since the tradesman was inspired by the Spirit he had no use for human learning. The same approach is taken by the author of *A Plain and Easy Road*, who ironically deprecated the Anglican insistence on an educated priesthood: 'And thus it happens that a cobler, thatcher, or ratcatcher gives as edifying puffs as any man of the most liberal education. Now this shows the folly of the Martinists' [Anglicans'] sending their youth to Oxf—d or C—b—ge. . . .' The author of *The Methodist*, after the Satanic spirits had entered the bosoms of the new preachers, saw ignorance explaining the mystery of God:

> Hence Ignorance of ev'ry Size,
> Of ev'ry shape Wit can devise . . .
> Shall yet pretend to keep the Key
> Of God's dark Secrets, and display

[7] T. B. Shepherd, *Methodism and the Literature of the Eighteenth Century*, p. 22.

His *hidden Mysteries*, as free
As if God's *privy Council* He,
Shall to his Presence rush, and dare
To raise *a pious Riot* there.

This ignorance in action is exemplified by Bickerstaff's Mawworm, turned preacher, who says: 'I have made several sermons already, I does them extrumpery, because I caun't write; and now the devils in our alley says, as how my head's turned.' Richard Graves's Geoffrey Wildgoose was better prepared than most lay preachers, or if a little learning is a dangerous thing, he was a greater threat than most. His theological training consisted of the reading of an old book containing 'a miscellaneous collection of godly discourses, upon predestination, election and reprobation, justification by faith, grace and freewill, and the like contraverted points of divinity. . . .'[8] The lay preacher of the satires, completely lacking in the training which would enable one to distinguish between heresy and orthodoxy or between superstition and a necessary belief, presumed to elucidate scriptural difficulties and to point the way to salvation.

In addition, Methodist preachers in general, not simply lay preachers, were also accused satirically of being in the profession for the sake of personal gain, and of taking advantage of their religious guise to seduce their female converts. Some satirists even attributed the seemingly irrational acts of the preachers to insanity. Undoubtedly the frequent appeals of Methodist preachers for funds for charity abetted the impression that they were avaricious. In the fashion of Chaucer's pardoner, the mock-preacher, modelled on Whitefield, directed his congregation: 'Riches are Thorns and Briars which obstruct your Passage to Heaven; I therefore have, in Compassion to your poor Souls, put you in a Way how to remove those Difficulties, by giving me your Money, *which is the Root of all Evil*. . . .'[9] Sir

[8] *The Spiritual Quixote*, I.17–18.
[9] *The Mock-Preacher*, p. 10. Many allegations were made about Whitefield's soliciting and misuse of funds, but these will be considered in the examination of the personal satire of Whitefield.

William Wealthy, in *The Methodist, a Comedy*, characterizes Squintum as 'An Enthusiastic Rascal!—That frightens the Ignorant out of their Wits, and afterwards picks their Pockets'.

But the attacks were principally upon the lay preachers. Colonel Lambert, in *The Hypocrite*, says: 'I own I cannot see with temper, sir, so many religious mountebanks impose on the unwary Multitude; wretches, who make a trade of religion, and shew an uncommon concern for the next world, only to raise their fortunes with greater security in this.' The author of *The Methodist* punned:

> The *Fishermen* no longer set
> For *Fish* the meshes of their Net,
> But catch, *like Peter, Men of Sin*,
> For *catching* is to *take them in*.

A mountebank doctor suggested to a Methodist preacher: 'I practice physick, and you preach the word: let us then fairly divide the credulous mob between us; the *fleece* is large enough for both.'[10] In Foote's *The Devil upon Two Sticks*, a young couple eloping with the devil's aid arrive in England and ask how they shall earn their living. Told by the devil that they should indulge in spiritual quackery and that if he were not the devil, he would choose to be a Methodist preacher, they demur, objecting momentarily to the rigorous lives they would have to lead. The devil tells them that the only sin they will have to avoid is simony. The definition he gives is an arresting one: 'Simony, Sir, is a new kind of canon, devised by these upstart fanatics, that makes it sinful not to abuse the confidence, and piously plunder the little property of an indigent man, and his family.'[11]

The anti-Methodists were quick to attribute immorality of all kinds—but particularly sexual—to the Methodist preachers.

---

[10] 'A Letter from a Mountebank Doctor to a Methodist Preacher', *The Gentleman's Magazine*, XXVIII (1758), p. 102.
[11] *The Dramatic Works of Samuel Foote, Esq.*, 2 vols (London, 1797), II.345-6.

Some of these accusations resulted from the nocturnal meetings of the Methodists and from the Methodist use of terms like the New Birth, but undoubtedly many were simply attempts to stigmatize a group of which the attacker disapproved. The author of *Methodism Triumphant*, in sonorous pseudo-Miltonic blank verse, was content to have his saint justify lying:

> N'er into Lying does their [the converts'] Language run;
> Unless to draw a Sinner from the Fiend;
> Or raise the Glory of the Sacred Band.
> If HOLY PAUL could wish himself accurs'd,
> To save a Remnant of the Hebrew Race;
> Well may the Modern Saint step from the Path
> Of rigid Verity, to save a World.

But other authors alleged that the preachers indulged in sexual immorality as they exercised their godly function. One non-satiric attack on the Methodists told of a Methodist who went mad because of lust but who since '... had turned father confessor, and forgave the *men their* sins for six pence each; as to the women, married or unmarried, *they* underwent the penance of *the lass to the frier*'.[12] The satiric attacks generally did not disguise the accusation under literary allusion, but they intensified it by a use of Methodist terminology and references to the supposedly godly character of the preachers. The author of *The Methodists, an Humorous Burlesque Poem* (1739) claimed that the Methodists, needing a group to support them, approach first the women. There the preachers meet with easy success:

> What *Maid* wou'd not be holy kist?
> Or who her Teacher can resist?
> Or when he tells her of her H - - - n
> What Blessings thence to all are giv'n, ...

[12] *A Letter to the Reverend Mr George Whitefield, Occasioned by His Remarks upon a Pamphlet, Entitled The Enthusiasm of Methodists and Papists Compared* (London, 1750), p. 16.

In those soft Moments, (all the Soul unbent)
The Maid on heavenly Joys intent,
Who could withstand the pleasing Proffer,
Or withstand the pious Lecher's Offer?
Say wou'd she not in her *New Birth*
Know some Part of her *Heav'n* on *Earth*?

The author of *Sketches for Tabernacle-Frames*, satirizing the doctrine of justification by faith, wrote:

Faith, Faith alone, 's the *Christian Church's* Banner,
And under *that* fight all the *Saints* that man her.
With *Man of God Priscilla* shares her *Bed*,
By *Christian Love* to *Prostitution* led. . . .

The author of an ironic attack on the Methodists, giving a dozen reasons why fortune tellers should be permitted to practice as other conjurers—including Methodists and Moravians—were, emphasized in reference to the fortune tellers: 'N.B. For the comfort of such of the fair sex, as may desire to consult us privately, we shall, like other conjurers, still continue to give them compleat satisfaction at our private apartments.'[13]

Finally the satirists, unable to account for the irrationality of the Methodist preachers, attributed it to insanity or, less frequently, to a lack of common sense. The earliest attack on the Methodists, 9th December 1732, had implied that the Oxford Methodists were insane: 'Among their own party they pass for religious persons, and men of extraordinary parts; but they have the misfortune to be taken by all, who have ever been in their company, for madmen and fools.'[14] James Lackington cited several instances of Methodist preachers foaming at the mouth and indulging in other actions conventionally allied to madness.

---

[13] 'A Dozen of Reasons Why the Sect of Conjurers, Called Fortune-Tellers, Should Have at Least as Much Liberty to Exercise Their Admirable Art, as Is Now Granted to Methodists, Moravians, and Various Other Sorts of Conjurers', *The London Magazine: or, Gentlemen's Monthly Intelligencer*, XXVI (1757), p. 484.
[14] Cited in Tyerman, *Life of Wesley*, I.86.

And he made much of the fact that the principal Methodist chapels in London, the Foundery and the Tabernacle, were in Moorfields, near Bethlehem Hospital, the famous hospital for lunatics: 'Some of these excellent preachers received the whole of their divine education in Moorfields, and in due time, after having given ample and satisfactory proofs of being properly qualified, have been admitted to professorships in the noble College situated on the south side of these fields, generally known by the name of *Bethlem*.' After he had gained his senses, Geoffrey Wildgoose, who foamed at the mouth as he preached, was characterized by Dr Greville as one who '... had been for some time under the influence of a deluded imagination'.[15] Oliver Goldsmith, sympathetic with Methodist oratorical reform, deplored the lack of common sense of the preachers: 'When I think of the Methodist preachers among us, how seldom they are endued with common sense, and yet how often and how justly they affect their hearers, I cannot avoid saying within myself, had these been bred gentlemen, and been endued with even the meanest share of understanding, what might they not effect!'[16]

The Methodist preachers thus were satirized as tradesmen who had left their proper jobs to perform tasks for which they were wholly unprepared. Their ignorance and their pretensions to inspiration were satirized. They were accused of being avaricious, immoral, and even insane.

Although the Methodist preachers were attacked extensively for the doctrines they preached, the manner in which they preached met with considerable criticism, since their bold new

[15] Graves, *The Spiritual Quixote*, I.27, II.275. An indication that some Methodist preachers were under Satanic influence is seen by W. Woolley, Chaplain of the Marshalsea, who, in referring to his mother's lack of credulity, said: 'This it was, no doubt, which prevented her from getting my nativity cast by a conjurer in our neighborhood, who having been for many years a *methodist preacher*, must have acquired a deeper knowledge of the *Black Art* than the mere student of *profane* astrology.' See *A Cure for Canting, or, The Grand Imposters of St Stephen's and of Surrey Chapels Unmasked: in a Letter to Sir Richard Hill, Bart.* (London, 1794), p. 17.

[16] *The Miscellaneous Works of Oliver Goldsmith, Including a Variety of Pieces Now First Collected*, ed. James Prior (Philadelphia, 1875), I.130.

way of preaching differed sharply from conventional practice. The average eighteenth-century sermon was read rather than preached and was delivered generally with little show of emotion. Oliver Goldsmith complained that much of the ignorance of the English lower class was due to its '... teachers, who with the most petty gentlemanlike serenity, deliver their cool discourses, and address the reason of men, who have never reasoned in all their lives'.[17] The Methodist sermon, on the other hand, was preached partially extemporaneously. It was many times a dramatic performance with the drama heightened by highly emotional language and direct appeals to the audience.

Despite some praise of oratorical reform undertaken by the Methodists, conservative voices were lifted to defend the old way of preaching and to protest against the new. The author of *A Serious Address to Lay-Methodists* (1745) affirmed: 'Their [the established clergy's] Preaching, tho' it may not be agreeable to the Taste of modern *Enthusiasts*, must be own'd to be grave, serious, and pathetic, without fanatical Flights.' Wesley aligned himself with the conservatives. He wrote to John King, one of his preachers in America: 'Scream no more at the peril of your soul. God now warns you by me whom He has set over you. Speak as earnestly as you can, but do not scream. Speak with all your heart, but with a moderate voice.'[18] If other preachers heeded Wesley's command, the satirists nevertheless belaboured them for their oratorical innovations, innovations which aroused the emotions of the hearers and made precise communication impossible.

The satirist emphasized the fact that the Methodist preacher by his flamboyant gestures and emotion-filled voice was appealing not to the reason or the judgement but to the emotions. The author of *Sketches for Tabernacle-Frames* asserted that Methodist preachers appeal to the passions to dupe their auditors:

[17] Ibid. I.128.
[18] Cited in Shepherd, *Methodism and the Literature of the Eighteenth Century*, p. 54.

> ... *strolling Knaves* will seldom *cant* or *preach*
> To *Judgements*—*there* they cannot make a Breach.
> No—to the *Passions* they address their *Tears*,
> And duping *those*, take *Asses* by the *Ears*. ...

Other satirists attributed to the preachers voices stentorian enough to wake the dead. Woolley, who compared a particular Methodist's voice to the blast of the trumpet at Judgement Day, depicted in unpleasant detail the fury into which a Methodist preacher worked himself: 'The big, round drops of sweat coursing one another down his hallowed front; and, in the heat of action, streams of blood sometimes gushing from his expanded nostrils;—his eyes starting;—his face on fire;—his mouth covered with holy foam;—his reverend locks disheveled; —his breast heaving like the billows in a tempest;—his left arm unfurling the banner of damnation against unbelievers, whilst his right seemed to brandish the bolt of divine wrath at their perverseness and incredulity'.[19] But probably the severest attack on Methodist oratory, that in *The Fanatic Saints* (1778), alleged that it was carefully planned. The author asserts that adults were trained at the Foundery, Wesley's London chapel, for their trade:

> In *holy Go-Carts* there, by *due Degrees*,
> They're taught to *snivel, groan, cant, whine,* and *wheeze,*
> *Heart-melting Tones* of *wheedling Intercession,*
> *Boanergy,* on *Mobs* to make Impression;
> *Stage-Tricks,* to fill the gloomy Soul with *Fear,*
> And wring from *Guilt* a *Shilling,* and a *Tear.*

Other attacks, like the song of Tony Lumpkin in Goldsmith's *She Stoops to Conquer*, attributed Methodist eloquence to liquor:

> When Methodist preachers come down,
> A preaching that drinking is sinful,
> I'll wager the rascals a crown,
> They always preach best with a skinful.

[19] *A Cure for Canting*, pp. 6–7. The preacher so characterized is probably Rowland Hill.

SATIRE OF METHODIST PREACHERS AND PREACHING

As more and more churches were closed to the Wesleys and to Whitefield, they began preaching in theatres, whatever other buildings were available, and even fields. By preaching in places other than churches, Methodists put themselves in a questionable legal position since field preaching was forbidden by the Conventicle Act of the Restoration, unless the service was held according to the liturgy and practice of the Church.[20] Presumably even meetings held according to the liturgy of the Church were permitted only at the discretion of the bishop in whose diocese they occurred. That Wesley was aware of the unusual nature of field preaching, as this practice was loosely called, is clear from his description of his first out-of-door sermon. He records in his *Journal* for 31st March 1739: 'In the evening I reached Bristol, and met Mr Whitefield there. I could scarce reconcile myself at first to this strange way of preaching in the fields, of which he set me an example on Sunday; having been all my life (till very lately) so tenacious of every point relating to decency and order, that I should have thought the saving of souls almost a sin if it had not been done in a church.' The use of lay preachers of course made field preaching necessary, since these were never permitted to preach in the churches.

The practice of preaching in the fields, along with that of itineration, with which it is closely related, met with bitter opposition.[21] Graves saw no need for either itineration or field preaching: '... our modern itinerant reformers, by the mere force of imagination, have conjured up the powers of darkness in an enlightened age. They are acting in defiance of human laws, without any apparent necessity, or any divine commission. They are planting the Gospel in a Christian country...[22] The field preacher, in the words of *The Celebrated Lecture on Heads*,

[20] Leslie F. Church, *The Early Methodist People* (2nd edn, London, 1949), p. 28. According to Albert D. Belden (*George Whitefield—The Awakener*) only one London pulpit was open to Whitefield in April 1739 (see p. 61).
[21] The practice of itineration is not being considered since there apparently was little satiric treatment of it, except for the fact that Nathaniel Snip, Geoffrey Wildgoose, and other fictional Methodist preachers were itinerants.
[22] *The Spiritual Quixote*, I.44.

'hath broken down Orthodox's [sic] bounds, and now riots on the common of Hypocrisy'. Other satirists simply drew scornful pictures of field preachers. Ezekiel Daw, in Cumberland's *Henry*, is characterized as 'one of those itinerant apostles called methodists, who preach *sub dio* to the country folks out of trees'. The author of *A Plain and Easy Road* asserted that Methodists would preach anywhere: 'Time, place, circumstances, *&c.*, make no difference;—the *Eolists* [Methodists] are above such low considerations as these;—their words are with power, either in a tabernacle—a *Martinist* temple [a church], if they can get there—from a cart—a butcher's stall—or the brink of a draw well.—'

Many anti-Methodists deplored in the Methodist sermons what they believed was an exaggeration of the pangs of hell in order to frighten people into godliness.[23] Wesley himself did not rely on the terrors of hell for his effectiveness as a preacher; his sermons, although they are designed to impress the emotions, are not minatory. But it is evident that an emphasis upon the necessity for conversion at the present moment could easily lead to a depiction of the horrors of Judgement Day. George Whitefield, the florid orator, was quite likely to preach such a sermon.

Theophilus Evans described non-satirically a hellfire Methodist preacher: 'The Preacher now grows more tempestuous and dreadful in his Manner of Address, stamps and shrieks, and endeavours all he can to increase the rising Consternation, which is sometimes spread over a great Part of the Assembly in a few Minutes from its first Appearance. And, to compleat the Work, the Preacher has his Recourse still to more frightful Representations; that *he sees Hell's flames flashing in their Faces:* and that they are *now! now! now! dropping into Hell! into the Bottom of Hell! the Bottom of Hell!*'[24]

The satiric descriptions of Methodist preaching are parallel.

---

[23] Obviously many of the orthodox clergy themselves preached as exuberantly frightening sermons as any of the Methodists, but the satirists nevertheless used the minatory sermon as characteristic of the Methodists.

[24] *The History of Modern Enthusiasm*, p. 119.

SATIRE OF METHODIST PREACHERS AND PREACHING

Nathaniel Snip, the tailor turned preacher, records: 'I preached the *New-Life*, the *Second Birth* to them, and threatened them with everlasting Brimstone and Fire in case they believed not themselves to be in a State of Perdition.'[25] The saint in Nathaniel Lancaster's *Methodism Triumphant* dramatically warns his audience of the uncertain duration of their lives:

> Hark! Hark! What is that deep, that awful Sound?
> It is the Knell of your departed Hours.
> Another portion of your time is gone:
> It bids you catch the favourable gale
> Of Opportunity: It bids you haste;
> Since on the Wing the minutes fly away,
> And never—never can they be recall'd.
> Soon will your days expire—perhaps this Night—
> Perhaps this Hour—Then ponder well this Truth—
> There is no GAOL-DELIVERY from Hell.

The fact that the Methodist sermon was delivered extemporaneously displeased many eighteenth-century conservatives, who saw this practice of depending upon the stimulation of the moment to provide inspiration for reflections upon the awesome subject of religion as an effrontery to God. Actually Methodist preaching was not completely extempore. Elliott-Binns notes: 'The preaching was . . . backed by intense conviction, but, at least for the leaders, it was not exactly extempore. They seem to have achieved a form which they found most effective; and the same sermon, or at least the same text, was used over and over again to different audiences, as can be seen from Wesley's journals.'[26] Interestingly Bickerstaff's Maw-worm preaches his sermons 'extrumpery' because he is illiterate.

The Methodists were severely satirized for the metaphoric boldness of their language in their everyday speech but

[25] *Journal of the Travels of Nathaniel Snip*, p. 10.
[26] *The Early Evangelicals*, p. 370. One of Charles Wesley's favourite texts was, 'Is it nothing to you, all ye that pass by?' which he used repeatedly through 1746–8.

particularly in their sermons. The anti-Methodist thought that it abounded too much in amorous terms, a little too reminiscent of the *Song of Songs*. John Free, after he had quoted a passage of religio-amorous language concerned with kisses and lambs, lamented: 'Pity! that such an *inspired* APOSTLE should prove so extravagantly *foolish* and *ridiculous*.

> He sends his wanton Lambs a *thousand* Kisses:
> Pray! to the *Masters?*—Sir, or to the *Misses?*'[27]

Geoffrey Wildgoose used metaphors to fit his audience: 'For the lewd and lascivious, he abounded with amorous expressions, and talked much in the nuptial style.'[28]

The Methodist reliance on scriptural quotation and allusions and the extensive use of the words *Jesus, Christ*, and the like deeply offended the non-Methodist. Some anti-Methodists believed that this stylistic device was intended to create an impression of extraordinary piety but that actually the scriptural quotations were so wrenched from their contexts that their meanings were destroyed.[29] George Crabbe, explaining in the preface to *The Borough* his reasons for including portraits of Methodists in his realistic depiction of a village, asserted that the sect clung to the peculiarities with which it had begun: '... there is the same offensive familiarity with the Deity ...; and there still remains the same wretched jargon, composed of scriptural language, debased by vulgar expressions, which has a kind of mystic influence on the minds of the ignorant.'[30] The editor of *A Fine Picture of Enthusiasm* suggested that the enthusiastic language concealed the lack of ideas and appealed to the emotions: 'The frequent mention of the *Name* of *Jesus*, the *Lamb of God*, and the Blood of *Jesus*, filling up great Part of their public Discourses, and very often only used to supply the *Want*

---

[27] John Free, *A Sermon Preached before the University at St Mary's in Oxford, on Whitsunday, 1758*, 2nd edn, (London, 1758), pp. 39–40.
[28] Graves, *The Spiritual Quixote*, I.84.
[29] See John Kirkby, *The Imposter Detected* (London, 1750), p. 1, and *Essay on the Character of Methodism*, pp. 16–17.
[30] George Crabbe, *Poems*, ed. A. W. Ward (Cambridge, 1905), p. 271.

of Ideas or sense; so that these Expressions *our Lord* Jesus Christ, the *Lamb of God*, and the *Blood*, the *precious Blood of our Lord* Jesus Christ, are used as the *Music* of their Discourses.'

The satirists generally put obvious paraphrases of the Scriptures into the mouths of Methodists. Ezekiel Daw, who, like St Paul and the Methodists, has a propensity for yearning at the bowels, says of Henry, the hero of the novel: 'He was guiltless, and we rescued him; friendless, and we protected him; hungry and we fed him; had he been in prison, I would have come unto him even there, for my bowels yearned toward him in Christian charity and compassion: and now, behold, he is brave; he wieldeth the sword against the enemies and blasphemers of his faith; he fighteth valiantly in the righteous cause of his king, his country, and his God.'[31] Mrs Snarewell, a procuress who has advertised through a pseudo register office for girls, bemoaning the fact that she doesn't have a virgin for a customer, is told to deceive him. She refuses in a unique reading of the Golden Rule: 'No, no ... if we expect to be Happy hereafter, we must endeavour to do, as we would be done by—'[32] Nathaniel Snip paraphrased the advice of Christ to His apostles as he wrote in his *Journal:* '*April* 3.—EARLY in the Morning I left *Hull.*—At my Departure I shook the Dust off my Shoes at them (Dirt I should have said, for in Truth it was wet Weather) in Token of my giving them over to their Vanity, and the Lust of the Flesh. ...'

Although many terms used by the Methodists, such as justification, regeneration, grace, salvation, and the like, were ridiculed by the anti-Methodists, no term was more ridiculed than the New Birth. The term, developed from the incident described in the third chapter of St John's Gospel of the visit of Nicodemus to Christ, was used by the Methodists to refer to the necessary conversion, which marked the Methodist's change

[31] Richard Cumberland, *Henry*, in *Ballantyne's Novelist's Library* (London, 1824), IX. 754.
[32] Joseph Reed, *The Register-Office: a Farce in Two Acts* (new edn, London, 1771), p. 33.

of life.[33] The term was seized upon for ridicule probably because it suggested childbirth. The most frequent satiric interpretation of the term is given in *The Spiritual Quixote*. When an hysterical girl comes to one of Geoffrey Wildgoose's meetings in Bristol, he mutters something about the New Birth. The girl's mother replies: 'But I have been very much terrified; and am sadly afraid my poor girl is with child.'[34] Another itinerant Methodist, Nathaniel Snip, encountering an old woman by the side of the road, begins to harangue her about the New Birth: '"*New Birth!*" replied she;—"Lord *help* me, *I have been past Child-bearing these many years.*"' The same Nathaniel Snip, referring indirectly to the term, says of one of the two converts he has won, a poor man named Brockally, whose livelihood was crying vegetables: 'Who knows but the Lord has marked this little *Nicodemus* out as one who shall stand before the Princes and Rulers of the Land, and instead of crying Oysters, &c., shall *cry aloud* the *mighty and wonderful Doings of the Lord*....' Other satirists simply held up the term to ridicule without developing it. For example, Mrs Cole, the procuress of *The Minor*, has experienced the New Birth. It was due, she says: '... to Mr. Squintum; who stept in with his saving grace, got me with the new birth, and I became, as you see, regenerate....'

The most effective satire of Methodist preachers, preaching, and the language used by the Methodists came in the parodies or descriptions of Methodist sermons. Here the satirists were able to depict the appalling ignorance of the preacher, his inflammatory style of preaching, and particularly the amorous pseudo-biblical language of Methodist sermons. A note in *The Fanatic Saints* (1778) describes such a sermon: 'One of these *blessed* Commentators, in an elegant Chapel, lately took for his Text the Falling of the *Manna*, which he said meant *electing Love* and *absolute Predestination*, and proved it to be *from all Eternity*: Thus *Manna*, we are told, said he, resembled *Coriander-Seed*,

---

[33] The pattern of that conversion will be examined in Chapter 6.
[34] *Op. cit.* II.33–4.

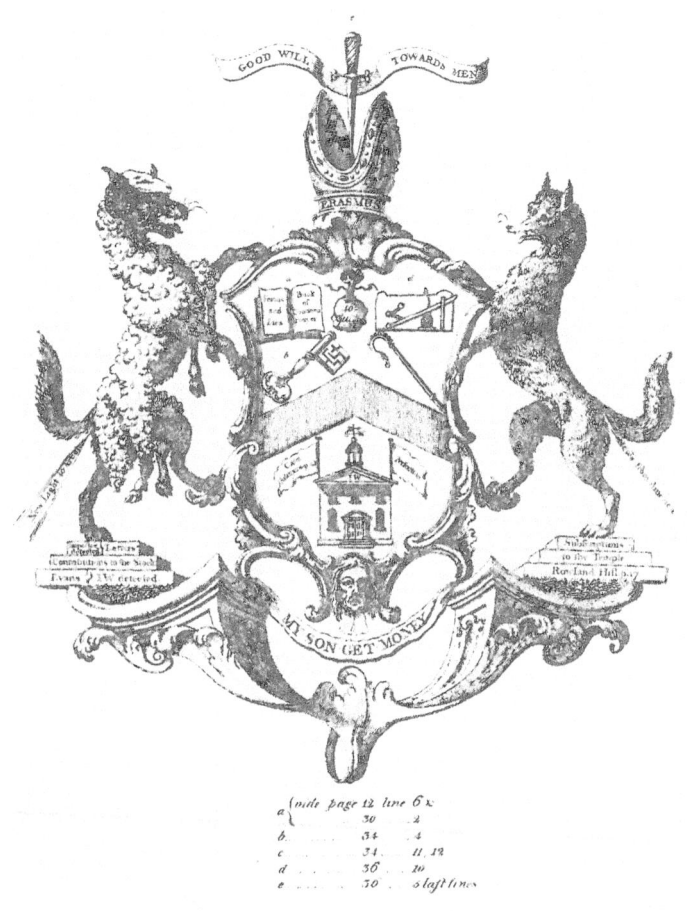

Frontispiece from *Perfection, A Poetical Epistle* (1778). The work, largely an attack on John Wesley, was '*Calmly* addressed to the greatest *Hypocrite* in England'.

which is round; what is *round* has neither *Beginning* nor End; and so, ye see, *Predestination* is *everlasting*.' But the most extensive parody of Methodist sermonizing came in *The Celebrated Lecture on Heads*. The sermon abounds in the allegedly characteristic Methodist devices: the use of Scriptural language and allusion, elaborate metaphor—more crude than that of the metaphysicals to which Dr Johnson objected—repetition for effect, and false etymologies. One of the righteous over much preaches:

Bretheren! Bretheren! Bretheren! The word bretheren comes from the Tabernacle, because we all breathe there-in—. . . Even as the cat upon the top of the house doth squall; even so, from the top of my voice will I bawl, and the organ pipes of my lungs shall play a voluntary among ye; and the sweet words that I shall utter, shall sugar candy over your souls, and make caraway comforts of your consciences. . . .—Give me a dram—Do give me a dram—A dram of patience I mean, while I explain unto you, what reformation, and what abomination mean! . . . Have you carried your consciences to the scowrers? Have you bought any fullers earth at my shop? to take the stains out? —You say, yes: you have! you have! you have!—But I say no: you lye! you lye!—I am no velvet mouth preacher; I scorn your lawn sleeve language—you are all full of filth. . . . Do put some money in the plate—Put some money in the plate;—and then all your iniquities shall be scalded away, even as they scald the bristles off the hog's back. . . .

Thus the eighteenth-century satirists generally depicted the Methodist preacher as a member of the lower class, often a cobbler or a tailor, who deserted his own trade and undertook preaching as an easy and lucrative way of obtaining a living. The preacher, as depicted in the satires, was illiterate or nearly so but clever enough to compound on the spur of the moment an emotional harangue made up of misquoted and misinterpreted passages from the Scriptures and an amorous vocabulary designed to titillate the audience. This he delivered with such force and vehemence that he frightened the crowd into conversion and made them ripe for fleecing. The Methodist preacher was in brief a clever rogue who had found a profitable livelihood.

CHAPTER FIVE

Satire of Methodist Practices

THE METHODIST use of unlicensed preachers, field preaching, and the like were Methodist practices which the anti-Methodists attacked severely. In addition to these was a host of practices, some trivial and some significant, which aroused the ire of the anti-Methodists. Such practices of the Methodists as keeping journals of their spiritual condition, singing hymns, and holding love-feasts and watch-night services the satirists found ridiculous and sometimes dangerous.

The regularity and 'method' of the lives of the members of the Holy Club at Oxford earned the eighteenth-century religious revival and the organization it conceived the lasting name of Methodist. Such activities as weekly communions, fasts on Wednesdays and Fridays, and regular hours for prayer made the name appropriate.[1] An element in the regularity of the Oxford Methodists and presumably of other Methodists later as well was the careful planning of the day. Wesley's account of his regular life on board ship bound for his missionary stay in Georgia may be taken as characteristic:

From four in the morning till five each of us used private prayer. From five to seven we read the Bible together, carefully comparing it (that we might not lean to our own understandings) with the writings of the earliest ages. At seven we breakfasted. At eight were the public prayers. . . . From nine to twelve I commonly learned German, and Mr Delamotte Greek. My brother writ sermons, and Mr Ingham read some treatise of

---

[1] The first known anti-Methodist attack in *Fogg's Weekly Journal* for 9th December 1732 singled out Methodist fasting. The death of William Morgan, one of the Oxford Methodists, in September 1732, was rumoured to have been caused by excessive fasting, and Wesley was forced to defend the practice to the boy's father.

divinity or instructed the children. At twelve we met to give an account to one another what we had done since our last meeting, and what we designed to do before our next. About one we dined. The time from dinner to four we spent with the people partly in public reading. . . . At four were the evening prayers. . . . From five to six we again used private prayer. From six to seven I read in our cabin to two or three of the passengers. . . . At seven I joined with the Germans in their public service. . . . At eight we met again, to exhort and instruct one another. Between nine and ten we went to bed, where neither the roaring of the sea nor the motion of the ship could take away the refreshing sleep which God gave us.[2]

Some of the satiric writers were amused by such methodical procedure and ridiculed the hour-by-hour planning of the day. Thus Lackington enumerated the events in his Methodist Sunday beginning with preaching at five o'clock in the morning and culminating in private devotions after eight in the evening.[3]

Part of the method of the Methodist lay in his keeping a record of his spiritual condition. The leaders of the movement—both the Wesleys and Whitefield—kept journals, and both John Wesley and Whitefield published portions of theirs during their lifetime. The practice of keeping a journal, Wesley said in the preface to the first edition of his *Journal*, resulted from his following the advice of Jeremy Taylor. Thus, wrote Wesley, '. . . I began to take a more exact Account than I had done before, of the manner wherein I spent my Time, writing down how I have employed every Hour'.[4] He apparently advocated keeping a journal as a matter of discipline.[5] At the 1744 Methodist Conference Wesley asserted that the Assistants should keep journals '. . . for our satisfaction as for the profit of their own souls'.[6]

[2] *The Journal of John Wesley*, I.112–13. Benjamin Ingham was one of the Oxford Methodists; Charles Delamotte, about whom little is known, had joined the missionaries at the last minute. The Germans were Moravians, whose influence on Wesley was profound.
[3] See above, p. 26.
[4] Op. cit. I.83.
[5] F. C. Gill, *The Romantic Movement and Methodism*, p. 79.
[6] T. W. Herbert, *John Wesley as Editor and Author*, p. 13.

Dr John Free, vicar of East Coker, Somerset, in 1758 ridiculed the pretentiousness and perhaps the excessive subjectivity of the Methodist practice of keeping a journal. In the preface to a sermon preached at Oxford he explained the origin of the term *Methodist*: 'The Name was first given to a few particular Persons, who affected to be so uncommonly *Methodical*, as to keep a Diary of the most insignificant and trivial Actions of their Lives; such perhaps, as how many Slices of *Bread* and *Butter* they eat with their *Tea*, how many *Dishes* of Tea they drank, how many *Country-dances* they called at their *Dancing-Club* or after a *Fast*, the Number of *Pounds* they might devour in a Leg of Mutton.'[7] One satirist depicted a Methodist trying to get into Elysium and carrying in his bosom a manuscript, which he reveals to be his journal: 'It's the *Journal* of my *Life*—of when I sung Psalms, when I *pray'd*, when I was *sick*, when I was *well*, when I *went*, when I *came*, when I *eat*, when I drank, when I *slept*—what I *saw*, and who I *saw*, and when I *saw*—what I *said*, and *he* said, and *she* said, and *they* said—and ten Million other *important* and *instructive* Actions of Life.'[8] A few critics as well accused the Methodists of rushing into print either with journals or with controversial religious pamphlets.[9]

One of the activities of the Methodist leaders almost from the beginning of the movement was the visiting of criminals condemned to death. A characteristic visit was one made by John and Charles Wesley to Newgate in November 1739. John Wesley describes it in these terms: 'On *Wednesday* [8 November] my brother and I went, at their earnest desire, to do the last good office to the condemned Malefactors. It was the most glorious instance I ever saw of faith triumphing over sin and death. One observing the tears run fast down the cheeks of one of them in particular, while his eyes were steadily fixed upwards, a few moments before he died, asked, "How do you feel your

---

[7] *A Sermon . . .*, p. vi.
[8] *The London Magazine: and Monthly Chronologer* [VIII] (1739), p. 451.
[9] Attacks on Whitefield's and Wesley's journals specifically will be considered in Chapters 7 and 8.

heart now?" He calmly replied, "I feel a peace which I could not have believed to be possible. And I know it is the peace of God, which passeth all understanding".'[10]

Lackington deprecated the joy which the converted felons possessed as they approached death: 'I have often thought that great hurt has been done to Society by the methodist preachers, both in town and country, attending condemned Malefactors, as by their fanatical conversation, visionary hymns, bold and impious applications of the scriptures, &c., many dreadful offenders against law and justice, have had their passions and imaginations so worked upon, that they have been sent to the other world in such raptures, as would better become martyrs innocently suffering in a glorious cause, than criminals of the first magnitude.' But other writers were apparently less disturbed by the effect of such visits on society. The author of *The Methodists, an Humorous Burlesque Poem* depicted the Methodists plaguing the wretches condemned to death. The unfortunate results of such a visit are demonstrated ironically when the Methodist Humphry Clinker, imprisoned on the charge of being a highwayman, a charge from which he is later exonerated, takes the opportunity to exhort his fellow prisoners. The turnkey complains: '"I don't care if the devil had him [Humphry]," said he; "here has been nothing but canting and praying since the fellow entered the place . . . the gentlemen get drunk with nothing but your damn'd religion. . . . I'll be damn'd if there's a grain of true spirit left within these walls; we shan't have a soul to do credit to the place, or make his exit like a true-born Englishman—damn my eyes! there will be nothing but snivelling in the cart; we shall all die like so many psalm-singing weavers."'[11]

[10] *Journal*, II.100. James Boswell reports that Dr Johnson, discussing the religious discipline appropriate for criminals, said: 'Sir, one of our regular clergy will probably not impress their minds sufficiently: they should be attended by a Methodist preacher, or a Popish priest.' *Boswell's Life of Johnson Together with Boswell's Journal of a Tour to the Hebrides and Johnson's Diary of a Journey into North Wales*, ed. George B. Hill, rev. edn, L. F. Powell (Oxford, 1934), IV.329.

[11] Smollett, *Works*, III.246.

METHODISM MOCKED

A practice of the Methodists publicized by both Methodists and anti-Methodists was the drawing of lots or opening the Bible at random to make decisions, both important and unimportant ones. Wesley used the device of drawing lots, perhaps borrowed from the Moravians,[12] notably in determining not to marry Sophia Hopkey; in advising Whitefield not to go as a missionary to Georgia; and in determining to preach and print his sermon on 'Free Grace', an action which did much to begin the Calvinist controversy.[13] One satirist stigmatized the practice as pagan, and another alleged that Wesley had chosen the doctrine of perfection by lot.[14] But other satirists showed Methodists using the practice. Geoffrey Wildgoose, the itinerant lay-preacher of *The Spiritual Quixote*, in deciding whether or not he will steal a horse, has '... recourse to our Bible, as Mr Wesley and Mr Whitfield have often done'.[15] But James Lackington demonstrated the ultimate ridiculousness of determining one's conduct by the practice. Locked in his room by his mistress to keep him from going to a Methodist meeting, he opened the Bible for advice. Finding there the verse 'He has given his angels charge concerning thee, lest at any time thou shouldst dash thy foot against a stone', Lackington interpreted it as an assurance of divine favour, whereupon he jumped out a third-story window and bruised his feet and ankles so severely that he was unable to work for a month.

One of the most important steps taken by the Methodists for the future organization of the movement was the formation of societies and the regulation of those societies. Strangely enough this Methodist practice was little satirized.[16] Geoffrey

---

[12] See Wesley, *Journal*, I.421 note, and Knox, *Enthusiasm*, pp. 411–12.
[13] See Wesley, *Journal*, I.325, 421 note.
[14] See *The Fanatic Saints: or, Bedlamites Inspired* (London, 1778), p. 35, and *Fanatical Conversion: or, Methodism Displayed* (London, 1779), p. 14.
[15] Op. cit. II.82.
[16] The absence of satires does not mean that the practice was approved of, but probably only that it did not provide a vivid, ready-made target for the satirists. Also religious societies had existed within the Church of England for a long time. But the attempts to force the Methodists to register as Dissenters are closely related to the attacks on the Methodist organization. See L. F. Church, *The Early Methodist People*.

Wildgoose, as he prepares to leave Gloucester, establishes in the Wesleyan manner a little society. James Lackington becomes the head of a spiritual community consisting of John Jones, his brother, Richard Jones, and his sister, Betsey Jones. A practice closely related to that of establishing societies was the recommendation of spiritual works to the members. This practice was common among the Methodists from the time of the Holy Club's planning to distribute copies of the *Whole Duty of Man* to Wesley's editing of the *Christian Library*. The fictional Nathaniel Snip recorded in his *Journal* in characteristic Methodist language a recommendation which he had made: 'To these newly-adopted Brethren I recommended the Perusal of a pious and devout Book which had been a great Instrument in saving my precious Soul; this Book was intitled and called, *A Pair of Stilts for a Dwarf in the Faith.*'

A frequent Methodist practice was that of praying over the sick. Wesley described a characteristic scene in his *Journal* for 31st March 1742: 'In the evening I called upon Ann Calcut. She had been speechless for some time; but almost as soon as we began to pray, God restored her speech: she then witnessed a good confession indeed. I expected to see her no more; but from that hour the fever left her, and in a few days she arose and walked, glorifying God.' Although Wesley did not definitely attribute the recovery to prayer, the satirists generally inferred from such descriptions a Methodist belief that miracles had been performed. Nathaniel Lancaster's saint in *Methodism Triumphant* directly asserts the power to work miracles:

> Oh! come and see, what miracles we work—
> Incurable Diseases how we cure—
> Legions of Devils how we exorcise;
> Or make them take possession, where we list.

Nathaniel Snip records in the fashion of Wesley and Whitefield an event parallel to Wesley's: '*April* 5.—This Morning I visited a Sister who lay dangerously ill of a Fever: What increased her Disorder was an inveterate Costiveness which bafled all the Art of the Doctor: I prayed by her, and sang an Hymn, which was no sooner ended, than it pleased the Lord in the Bowels of his Compassion to open her Bowels: on this she recovered so surprizingly as to be well in two Days Time:— Oh, the great Power of Prayer.'

The Methodist insistence upon the virtuous conduct of all members of Methodist societies and the regular examination of the individual members laid the movement open to the charge of popery. The examination of individuals was seen as parallel to Roman Catholic confession. While certainly detailed examation went on, Wesley in his *Journal* described it only in general terms. On 7th April 1741 he wrote that he had examined the society in London: 'In the evening, having desired all the bands to meet, I read over the names of the United Society, and marked those who were of a doubtful character, that full inquiry might be made concerning them. On *Thursday*, at the meeting of that society, I read over the names of these, and desired to speak with each of them the next day, as soon as they had opportunity. Many of them afterwards gave sufficient proof that they were seeking Christ in sincerity. The rest I determined to keep on trial, till the doubts concerning them were removed.' Leslie Church asserts that the development of the class meeting as a place for the discussion of problems was compared to the confessional.[17]..

The satirists generally emphasized the similarity between the Methodist practice and Roman Catholicism. The Methodist converts unlocked their souls and were absolved by tailors; the Methodist leaders, characterized as 'Sons of Loyola' and 'Bedlam-Popes', used confession to discover willing penitents and to

[17] Ibid. p. 157. The class, first developed in 1742, was made up of about a dozen members and was originally designed to remove indebtedness on a Methodist building, but was later used as a basic unit of the Methodist organization. See Wesley, *Journal*, II.528. Class leaders were required to be able to answer such questions concerning their members as: 'Does this and this person in your class live in drunkenness or any outward sin? Does he go to church, and use the other means of grace? Does he meet you as often as he has opportunity?' (Wesley, *Journal*, III.285).

keep control over the members.[18] The author of *A Plain and Easy Road* explained the real value of confession: 'As a shepherd, by his crook, has his sheep within his reach, and he can pull them to this side, thrust them from him, or bring them back; so by the dint of confession, Mr —— has his followers under his thumb; and where, I pray you, can they be safer?' Although Lackington satirized Methodist confession, he saved most of his ridicule for the penitent. Of an old man who confessed in a meeting of the band that he had been tempted to seduce his maid, he wrote: 'I could not help thinking the old gentleman was right in charging it *on the devil*, as there was little reason to think it was any temptation of *the flesh.*'

Apart from the use of unlicensed preachers, the holding of love-feasts and watch-night services was probably the Methodist practice most roughly handled. The love-feast, modelled on the *Agape* of the early Church, had been taken over from the Moravians. George Eayrs, a Methodist historian, asserts that the feasts, open originally only to members of the bands—i.e. those who were justified—but later open to all society members, served plain cake and water, which '. . . was followed by testimonies concerning His love to them and theirs to Him, interspersed with songs of praise'.[19] The Methodists probably expected accusations of sexual immorality to be made about nocturnal meetings and sought to regulate them carefully, since Tyerman notes that the Conference of 1765 stated that a love-feast should not last for more than an hour and a half, permitting every one to be at home by nine.[20] But its name and the fact that it took place at night caused the love-feast to be identified with sexual immorality.

Such immorality is intimated in the title of a satire, attributed to Laurence Sterne, *A Funeral Discourse Occasioned by the Much*

[18] See *Fanatic Saints*, pp. 7–8; *Fanatical Conversion*, p. 19; and *Perfection. A Poetical Epistle. Calmly Addressed to the Greatest Hypocrite in England* (London, 1778), pp. 21–3.
[19] *A New History of Methodism*, ed. W. J. Townsend, H. B. Workman, and George Eayrs (Nashville, n.d.), I.286.
[20] Tyerman, *Life of Wesley*, II.539.

METHODISM MOCKED

Lamented Death of Mr Yorick, ... Preached before a Very Mixed Society of Jemmies, Jessamies, Methodists and Christians at a Nocturnal Meeting in Petticoat Lane. ... But other satirists, like the author of *The Love-Feast* (1778), left no doubt about their accusations. The Methodists meet at night for sexual orgies:

> *There* Saints, *new-born*, lascivious *Orgies* hold,
> Meek *Lambs* by *Day*, at *Night* no *Wolves* so bold,
> There the *new Adam* tries the *old one's* Fort,
> And *Children of the Light* in *Darkness sport.* ...

The Methodist leaders use aphrodisiacs in the wine of the Eucharist;[21] the unfettered licentiousness does not stop at incest:

> Together wanton pairs promiscuous run,
> *Brothers* with *Sisters*, *Mothers* with a *Son:*
> *Fathers*, perhaps with yielding *Daughters* meet,
> And *Converts* find their *Pastor's* Doctrines sweet;
> *Pure Souls* are fir'd by *Love's* divinest Spark
> And *Paradise* is open'd in the *Dark.*[22]

The watch-night service, a peculiarly Methodist practice, was originated by the Kingswood colliers who after their conversion spent in prayer the Saturday nights that they had normally spent in drunkenness.[23] The first London watch-night service is described by Wesley on 9th April 1742:

We commonly choose for this solemn service the Friday night nearest the full moon, either before or after, that those of the congregation who live at a distance may have light to their several homes. The service begins at half an hour past eight,

---

[21] *The Love-Feast. A Poem* (London, 1778), p. 28. Although the author did not actually call what he described a celebration of the Eucharist, he used the term *chalice*, which was undoubtedly intended to suggest the sacrament. The Eucharist was normally not celebrated at love-feasts. The charge of the use of aphrodisiacs, the author of *Fanatical Conversion* asserted, was supported by the solemn declaration of a 'reformed Methodist Preacher'. See p. 25.
[22] *The Love-Feast*, p. 28.
[23] Wesley, *Journal*, II.536 note.

and continues till a little after midnight. We have often found a peculiar blessing at these seasons. There is generally a deep awe upon the congregation, perhaps in some measure owing to the silence of the night, particularly in singing the hymn, with which we commonly conclude:

> Hearken to the solemn voice,
> The awful midnight cry!
> Waiting souls, rejoice, rejoice,
> And feel the Bridegroom nigh.

This service was later held only on 31st December.[24]

The satirists alleged, much as they had done for the love-feasts, that the watch-night services cloaked sexual immorality. The author of *Fanatical Conversion* implied that the length of the service was designed to heighten the pleasure of the converts through anticipation. The noise from such services, he alleged, came from maddened sinners who could scarcely wait for grace, from yielding saints whom 'John's Exorcists' were to make pregnant sinners. At the watch-night service, the author of *Perfection* asserted:

> ...*preaching* LUBBERS, who have dropp'd their PACK;
> In *watch-night Labours* prove themselves not slack,
> Thro' *Calls of Love* to tender Scenes advance,
> And slide into *Adult'ry* in a Trance?

The satirists of the love-feast and the watch-night service aimed at a single target, sexual immorality.

Interestingly enough the Methodist practice of singing hymns won for the Methodists a considerable notoriety. The use of hymns helped to isolate the Methodists from their neighbours, since the use of hymns was confined almost entirely to dissenters.[25] Townsend writes: 'So strong was the prejudice against these "human hymns" as contrasted with the metrical "Psalms

---

[24] Townsend, *et al.*, I.290.
[25] Shepherd, *Methodism and the Literature of the Eighteenth Century*, p. 25, and Townsend, *et al.*, I.245.

of David", that even the paraphrases of Dr Watts, which, except in their superior literary grace, only departed from the manner of the metrical versions by giving a New Testament interpretation to the original psalm, were looked upon with grave suspicion, and maintained a precarious and constantly challenged position.'[26] Yet the Methodists wrote and translated hymns and in some cases set them to secular tunes. There is, for example, a story that Charles Wesley persuaded a group of sailors to sing a hymn 'by composing words to fit the music-hall tune, "Nancy Dawson".'[27] The use of such hymns was an integral part of the Methodist experience.

The anti-Methodist attack on the Methodist hymns blamed both words and tune. Both were considered unsuitable artistically and spiritually for religious services. One anti-Methodist characterized the hymns as 'the extravagant and unmeaning rhapsodies of their [the Methodists'] own bad *poets*, and worse divines'. Another objected that the hymns were too emotional 'so that their *Singing* is calculated to engage the *Passions* by nothing more than Words, and the Melody of the Sounds, or Voices. . . .'[28] The author of *The Love-Feast* said of Methodist hymns:

> In *Hymns* they take th' Almighty by the Nose;
> Ev'n of his *Oath* upbraid him with a *Breech*
> *Omniscience* daringly presume to teach. . . .

John Kirkby commented on a Methodist hymn entitled 'A Prayer for One That Is Lunatic': 'Did ever Mortal hear such Rant put up by People in their Wits, by Way of Prayer to God for the Distressed? . . . it seems, these inspired *Methodists* conceive no Method more proper to apply to Heaven in the Behalf of a mad Person, than by acting as if they were stark mad

---

[26] Townsend, *et al.*, I.245. Townsend explains the popularity of the Wesleyan hymns by the fact that they were used in services which were not designed to replace the services of the Church.
[27] Herbert, *John Wesley as Editor and Author*, p. 69.
[28] *Letter to the Rev. Mr M--re B--k-r*, pp. 16-17; *Fine Picture of Enthusiasm*, p. 24.

themselves.' A William Riley protested that the Methodists had begun to introduce their tunes into the churches. He admitted, however: 'It is true they have not yet ventured to sing Ballad-Tunes, as at the Tabernacle, Foundery, and elsewhere; because by such a Proceedure they would doubtless be forbid the Use of the Church, but the Tunes they commonly use are generally too light and airy for Church-Music, and consequently have nothing in their composure that may excite a true Spirit of Devotion.'[29] He denied that the Methodists had made any improvements in religious singing and asserted that '. . . all judicious and well-meaning People, . . . doubtless will condemn such Practices as profane and irreligious, or, as the wild Chimeras of a distempered Brain'. Thomas Chatterton asserted that the composition of Wesley's hymns was so odd that 'You'd swear 'twas bawdy songs made godly'.[30]

Generally the anti-Methodists depicted the Methodists as singing through their noses and with sanctimonious countenances. A mountebank doctor promises a Methodist preacher that his assistant will aid the preacher: '. . . he may afterwards assist you in *setting a hymn of your own composing:* I can assure you, he has an admirable talent this way, can *twang* it through his nose very harmoniously, and put on as sanctified a face as any of your profession.'[31]

Finally the anti-Methodists alleged that the Methodists departed from Anglican liturgical practice. The Methodist ministers, in the words of the author of *An Earnest and Affectionate Address to the People Called Methodists* (1745), 'set aside and altered the Liturgy at their Pleasure'. While there were occasional attacks on such practices as extempore praying, the centre of the attack on liturgical practice was the Holy Communion. From the early days of Methodism when the Holy Club was in

[29] William Riley, *Parochial Music Corrected* (London, 1762), p. 3.
[30] Thomas Chatterton, *The Poetical Works of Thomas Chatterton*, ed. W. W. Skeat (London, 1905), I.193. See also *The Poetical Works of Thomas Chatterton* (Boston, 1855), pp. 29–30.
[31] *The Gentleman's Magazine*, XXVIII (1758), p. 102.

existence at Oxford, the rigorous Methodists had emphasized weekly communions. Throughout his life John Wesley stressed frequent communion.[32] Partly because the Methodists emphasized the sacrament so much, the attacks, not primarily satire, centred upon it and stressed Methodist deletions from the liturgy. The author of *A Review of All the Doctrines Taught by the Rev. Mr John Wesley* accused Wesley of omitting the general confession from the Communion service, 'no doubt, as ill suiting so angelic a company'. A milder attack asserted that Methodist ministers, as they distributed the elements, said only the words, '*The body of our Lord Jesus Christ*, and *The Blood of our Lord Jesus Christ*', and left out the remainder of what the rubric prescribes to be said. By omitting the words, 'Take and eat this in remembrance that Christ died for thee, and feed on him in thy heart by faith, with thanksgiving', the Methodists, the author implied, were trying to introduce a belief in transubstantiation.[33]

Other writers were moved to comment upon the attitude of Methodist communicants approaching the sacrament. The country gentleman, who wrote *A Letter to the Rev. Mr M - - re B - - k - r*, indignantly asked: 'Did not a methodist propose this question to *your son* and many others, as they were approaching the table to receive the holy sacrament, *What condition is your soul in?* with several other interrogatories, equally unseasonable and impertinent.' Bishop Lavington generally approved of the Methodists' devotion at the Communion, although he saw the ecstasy into which some communicants fell as enthusiastic and Popish.[34]

Yet the anti-Methodists did object to other liturgical irregu-

---

[32] Henry Carter, *The Methodist Heritage*, p. 103. I have included the attacks on the liturgical practices of the Methodists, although they are not primarily satiric, in order to make the summary of the reaction to Methodist practices as nearly complete as possible.

[33] [A. B.] *An Earnest and Affectionate Address to the People Called Methodists* (2nd edn, London, 1745), p. 35. The quotation of the liturgy comes from the American Book of Common Prayer.

[34] [George Lavington] *The Enthusiasm of Methodists and Papists Compar'd* (London, 1749), p. 132.

larities of the Methodists. Thomas Green, vicar of Wymeswould, Leicestershire, saw in the practice of extempore praying an impious affront to God: 'But when persons appear before God in public to offer whatever comes into their mind, this is, I think, making too free with the divine majesty.'[35] The author of *A Letter to the Rev. Mr M - - re B - - k - r* attacked Methodist prayers for the dead: 'Mr *Wesley*, in his prayers for every day in the week, makes use of these extraordinary words, "lastly, I commend to thy mercy the souls of all that are departed this life in thy true faith and fear". This is a very *popish* prayer to be used by a protestant divine.' But these attacks are widely scattered.

In general the satirists of Methodist practices ridiculed the pretentiousness of Methodist actions. They depicted the keeping of a journal of one's spiritual ups and downs as the foolish recording of the trivial events of one's life; they depicted the opening of the Bible at random to determine important actions as an absurd and irrational act which resulted in absurd and irrational consequences; but above all they depicted the Methodist love-feast and watch-night services, non-public meetings at which the Methodist flocks were strengthened in the faith, as private meetings limited to those willing converts who desired to be joined in the flesh.

[35] *A Dissertation on Enthusiasm* (London, 1755), p. 34. Thomas Jackson, a nineteenth-century biographer of Charles Wesley, notes that in the administration of the Holy Communion, Charles Wesley 'always used the form contained in the Book of Common Prayer; but he did not confine himself to it. He was often drawn out largely in extemporary prayer' (p. 466).

CHAPTER SIX

Satire of Methodist Converts and Conversion

THE METHODIST practices of itineration and field preaching were designed to carry an evangelical Protestant Christianity to the religiously ignorant, or in terms more characteristic of eighteenth-century Methodism, to carry the gospel to the unenlightened. The ultimate goal was the acceptance of that gospel by the ignorant, the enlightenment of the unenlightened. That the gospel was accepted by the individual was indicated by an experience, more or less remarkable, called conversion. In this experience the individual saw the futility of his life, recognized his sinfulness, and submitted himself completely to God. The kind of person to whom the Methodist preacher successfully appealed and the religious experience, the conversion, which the newborn Methodist underwent were repeatedly satirized.

Methodism, in its beginnings at Oxford, necessarily appealed to a relatively limited and intellectually aristocratic audience. But when John Wesley announced that he took the world for his parish, the movement had obviously enlarged its appeal. Although some notable aristocratic converts were made—the Countess of Huntingdon particularly—the Methodists were most successful among those whom the Church had not previously reached, the lower class. Later historians have recognized that the eighteenth-century Methodists were drawn largely from the uneducated labouring class, although the full-time ministers of the first two generations of Methodism, presumably the cream of the converts, came from a single group between the middle class and unskilled labourers and few were from the lowest economic group.[1] The movement apparently did not appeal primarily to the emotionally immature, or as the century was fond of pointing out, to the feeble-minded and the insane, for Sydney Dimond, after examining Methodist conversions in the eighteenth century, concludes that '... a large proportion of the subjects are adults, and they are not unstable or neurotic types'.[2]

At the same time that the conservative anti-Methodist would undoubtedly have recognized that the Methodist appeal was primarily to the uneducated lower class, he saw other groups which for various reasons were easily converted to the new enthusiasm.

The satirists, believing that the emotions of women were more easily swayed than those of men, feared that women, like Eve in Paradise, were particularly subject to the temptation of Methodism. The author of *The Methodists, an Humorous Burlesque Poem* alleged that the Methodists formed the nucleus of their group with women, who could be easily swayed. James Lackington said of Wesley's followers: '... I believe that by far the greatest part of his people are females; and not a few of them sour, disappointed old maids, with some others of less prudish disposition.' Lancaster in *Methodism Triumphant* asserted that of the 24,000 converts his saint has won, most are females. Other satirists accused the Methodists of pleading to women for funds so successfully that they robbed their husbands' pockets. Mr Ranter, in *The Spiritual Minor*, tells of a woman who robbed her husband of forty guineas to give Dr Squintum. A cobbler's wife in *The Mock-Preacher*, who has given away all their money to the preacher, is beaten by her husband, but fellow female converts, learning the reason for her beating, rush to her aid. The author of *Ranae Comicae Evangelizantes*, a

---

[1] Wellman J. Warner, *The Wesleyan Movement in the Industrial Revolution* (London, 1930), pp. 166, 250. See also Hoxie N. Fairchild, *Religious Trends in English Poetry* (New York, 1939, 1942, 1949), II.91.

[2] Sydney G. Dimond, *The Psychology of the Methodist Revival* (London, 1926), p. 162.

curious attack upon all religion, summarizing the effects of a fanatic preacher upon his audience, envisioned a serious future danger because so many of the converts were female: 'Several of them communicated, no doubt, to the fruit of their womb, the dire contagion of superstition, and stamp'd th' unhappy foetus a fanatic for life.'[3]

Other attacks alleged that the Methodist preachers had a remarkable success in converting prostitutes because a religious faith, like Methodism, which denied the value of works presumably did not require any renunciation of their enjoyment or profit. This is almost the explanation which a character in Foote's *The Minor* gives for the success of the Methodists: 'No wonder these preachers have plenty of proselytes, whilst they have the address so comfortably to blend the hitherto jarring interests of the two worlds [the carnal and the spiritual].' The orator in *A Plain and Easy Road* complains that the Martinist or Anglican road is much too narrow, that it excludes such basically devout people as bawds: 'The *Martinists* (*bad* as their way is) are too partial in their admission of travellers into it; whereas our turnpike [the Eolist or Methodist] refuses none:— The bawd, and her customers, male and female—who (whilst they remain'd reprobates) were continually pester'd, plagu'd, teas'd, perplex'd, and hurried out of their lives, by a certain intruding thing call'd *conscience*, and contrary to the directions in their ancestor's will [the Scriptures], (now become *Eolists*) are happily delivered from that slavery, and find that their doings are now no ways contradictory to the—mystical—meaning of it at least.' Other satirists depicted the new Eve as plying the old one's trade. Corinna in *The Love-Feast*, converted, follows her calling among the Methodists:

> *Corinna*, (from the *Magdalen* a *Stray*)
> Tir'd of *unsocial Pennance* broke away:
> *Perfection* sets her free to sin again;

[3] *Ranae Comicae Evangelizantes: or, The Comic Frogs Turned Methodist* (London, 1786), p. 43.

She plies the *F[ound]ry* now, and *Drury-Lane*.
All *Saints* agree the *F - - ry* yields by far
More *Culls* than *Ludgate-Hill* or *Temple-Bar;*
Its *Festivals* devoutly *she* attends,
For *there* she finds *Salvation* and *old Friends*.

Shamela's mother, in Fielding's novel, herself a whore, is fond of Whitefield's writings. She writes her daughter: 'I have inclosed you one of Mr. *Whitefield's* Sermons, and also the Dealings with him. . . .'[4] The typical Methodist convert in the satires is a whore or a brothel-keeper, like Mrs Cole, in *The Minor*.

The satirists saw the Methodist denial of the value of good works appealing to other kinds of people: certain sinners (hypocrites, drunkards, adulterers) and criminals (extortioners, thieves, and murderers). These, like the prostitutes, did not have to reform. According to the author of *A Plain and Easy Road* the Eolists [Methodists] are assured '. . . upon the *bona fide* of our holders-forth, that fornicators, adulterers, and effeminate, can *now* enter into a state of bliss; together with thieves, drunkards, and extortioners; that these are *indeed* the properest people to be transplanted hither, and that the road was both widened and made good, chiefly for their use'. Most of those who come to hear Lancaster's saint are stained with vice. This view of the Methodist appeal reaches the peak of irony in the *Journal of the Travels of Nathaniel Snip* when the tailor-preacher finds that the people of Wighton are too good to be converted to Methodism. He records in his *Journal:* 'Good Works are apt to make Men proud, and are often a Bar to their applying for a *Saving Grace*.—Had they been Murderers, Adulterers, &c., there might have been some Hopes:—'Tis such as these make the best Christians. . . .'

The satirists also alleged that the old, frightened by approaching death, were likely to be beguiled to Methodism in an

[4] Fielding, *Shamela*, p. 23. The 'Dealings' is a reference to the early Whitefield autobiography: *An Account of God's Dealings with the Reverend Mr George Whitefield* (1740). The reference also implies that the whore has served Whitefield in a professional capacity.

attempt to make their peace with God. After suggesting numerous reasons for the conversion to Methodism of a group of women, Francis Coventry then wrote of one of his characters, Lady Harridan: '... having worn out her life in vanity, cards, and all sorts of luxury, [she] was now turned methodist at seventy, and thought by presenting heaven with the dregs of her age, to atone for all the riot and lasciviousness of her youth. For this purpose she had renounced all public diversions, put herself under the tuition of the two great field-preaching apostles, and was become one of the warmest votaries of that prevailing sect.'[5] But an old man depicted in *The Love-Feast* apparently became a Methodist in order to enjoy rather than to renounce as Lady Harridan had done.

Finally, the satirists depicted the Methodists as appealing to various groups and types of people for converts. Lackington non-satirically characterized most of the Methodist converts as '... very ignorant, (as is the case with enthusiasts of every religion)'. Of his own brief career as a Methodist, he implied that the Methodist appeal was largely to adolescents and other immature persons when he wrote that he was a Methodist from the time he was fifteen until he was twenty-one. Lancaster, in *Methodism Triumphant*, satirizing the location of the Foundery in Moorfields, suggested that the converts came from Bethlehem Hospital. But probably John Harman, who had attempted to explain Whitefield's success through the confluence of the stars, provided the most nearly unique delineation of the kind of person who became a Methodist convert. Methodism was governed by Saturn, and the Methodists were, according to him, Saturnians:

... Saturn is the author of melancholy and malevolence; those persons delight to live alone, to lead a miserable, solitary, and abstemious life; they take no delight in pleasing sports and recreations; their delight is to live in dark places, caves, dens,

[5] Francis Coventry, *The History of Pompey the Little, or The Life and Adventures of a Lap-Dog*, intro. Arundell del Re (Waltham, Saint Lawrence, 1926), pp. 76–7.

SATIRE OF METHODIST CONVERTS AND CONVERSION

holes, places where men have been buried, muddy or dirty, stinking and filthy places; they love night rather than day, darkness rather than light, and chuse plain and mean apparel. . . . They are chiefly for their own ends, seducing people to their opinion, full of revenge and malice, little caring for the church or religion: he also represents Monks, Jesuits, and other Sectaries. This short account of what has been found to be the nature of this Planet, may a little enlighten you as to the principles of Methodists.[6]

Yet one satire makes Squintum boast to Foote that the preacher has converted all sorts and conditions of men:

> I have 'em in thousands, Sam Foote, at my heel.
> The cobler, the countess, the bishop must feel.[7]

The heterogeneous groups which made up the Methodist converts—women, prostitutes and other evil livers, the old, the ignorant, and the young—were actually composed of only two kinds of people: those who were gulled and those who wished to use religion for their own ends.

Few things about Methodism offended the non-Methodist quite as much as the Methodist conversion, since the Methodist alleged that this brief emotional experience transformed him miraculously, instantaneously, from the worst of sinners, by his own admission, to the best of Christians. If this irrational assertion were not enough to offend the anti-Methodist, this experience by which the Methodist was made aware that he was a sinner, that he trusted in Christ for his salvation, and finally that he was assured of the forgiveness of his past sins was so often accompanied by faintings, fits, and other irrational behaviour that the non-Methodist, at first startled, was soon horrified at the attribution of these abnormal physical actions to the Holy Spirit.

The conversion, generally considered necessary in some form or other by the Methodists, varied from the mild experience of

[6] *Remarks upon the Life, Character and Behaviour of the Rev. George Whitefield* . . ., pp. 20–1.
[7] *A Letter of Expostulation from the Manager of the Theatre in Tottenham-Court, to the Manager of the Theatre in the Hay-Market* (London, n.d.), p. 4.

John Wesley to the ecstatic and violently physical one of Thomas Maxfield. Wesley described his very restrained one in his *Journal* for 24th May 1738: 'In the evening, I went very unwillingly to a society in Aldersgate Street, where one was reading Luther's preface to the *Epistle to the Romans*. About a quarter before nine, while he was describing the change which God works in the heart through faith in Christ, I felt my heart strangely warmed. I felt I did trust in Christ, Christ alone for salvation; and an assurance was given me that He had taken away *my* sins, even *mine*, and saved *me* from the law of sin and death.' Wesley's description of Thomas Maxfield's conversion on 21st May 1739 comes as a part of the description of other conversions. Yet the passage reveals clearly what the conservative objected to:

In the evening I was interrupted at Nicholas Street, almost as soon as I had begun to speak, by the cries of one who was 'pricked at the heart', and strongly groaned for pardon and peace. Yet I went on to declare what God had already done, in proof of that important truth, that He is 'not willing *any* should perish, but that *all* should come to repentance'. Another person dropped down... a little boy... was seized in the same manner. A young man who stood up behind fixed his eyes on him, and sunk down himself as one dead; but soon began to roar out and beat himself against the ground, so that six men could scarcely hold him. His name was Thomas Maxfield. ... Meanwhile many others began to cry out to the 'Saviour of all', that He would come and help them, insomuch that all the house (and indeed all the street for some space) was in an uproar.

Although these strong physical reactions did not seem to occur in Wesley's congregations after the early forties, they were considered throughout the century to be a characteristic part of the conversion experience.[8]

[8] Dimond asserts that the abnormal behaviour of Wesley's audience occurred only between 1739 and 1742 (see *The Psychology of the Methodist Revival*, p. 126). Umphrey Lee, on the other hand, notes that the screaming and dropping down as if dead rarely occurred after 1739 (*The Lord's Horseman* [New York, 1954], p. 86). Strangely enough, Whitefield's audiences suffered fewer physical reactions than Wesley's. Albert D. Belden attributes this to the fact that Whitefield's oratory relieved vicariously their emotion (*George Whitefield: The Awakener*, p. 269).

SATIRE OF METHODIST CONVERTS AND CONVERSION

The anti-Methodist objected strenuously to the Methodist insistence that such a conversion had to occur. One author insisted that the violent pangs of the New Birth were characteristic only of the conversions of the wicked: 'Persons, who have had a pious Education from their Childhood, should not make themselves uneasy, because they cannot give any very particular and precise Account of the *Time* and *Manner* of their *Conversion*, or *second Regeneration*. . . .'[9] He and others saw unfortunate results of this insistence upon a conversion. He believed that it caused some Christians to despair: 'Modern Enthusiasts carry their Fancies of Instantaneous and Irresistible Grace *so* far, as to suffer *all* Religion to *rest* upon this *one* Point; and *poor, pious, melancholy* Christians, who *cannot* work themselves up into *such* Heights, are delivered either to *Despair* or *Madness*.'[10] James Lackington alleged that this despair made many give up all religion and morality and sink 'into the abyss of vice and wickedness'.

The satirists treated this assumption that all individuals must undergo such a conversion in order to be truly Christian in various ways. In *Humphry Clinker* the giddy Lydia Melford, writing to her friend Letty, sees her failure to be converted as an indication that she is damned: 'I was persuaded to go to the Tabernacle, where I heard a discourse that affected me deeply—I have prayed fervently to be enlightened, but as yet I am not sensible of these inward motions, these operations of grace, which are the signs of a regenerated spirit; and therefore I begin to be in terrible apprehensions about the state of my poor soul.[11] Other writers ironically suggested both that one conversion was all anyone ever needed to pardon any iniquities that he wished to engage in and that one might be converted each time he sinned. The author of *A Plain and Easy Road* has his Methodist apologist say: 'In this respect his [the orator's] sensible scheme differs very much from the *Martinists;* that whereas they require

[9] *A Letter from a Clergyman*, p. 5.   [10] Ibid. p. 41.
[11] Smollett, *Works*, III.221.

their followers to grunt and groan, and bewail their iniquities, every time they commit them; once is sufficient for us, if it be done so *heartily* at the tabernacle as to produce fits; then it is that we are eased of our burdens, past—present—and to come—...' But Bishop Lavington in *The Enthusiasm of Methodists and Papists Compar'd* suggested that Methodists, repenting each time they sinned, might have a daily New-Birthday.

The anti-Methodist, and specifically the satirist, saw definite natural causes for the Methodist conversions, ridiculed the pattern of them, and prophesied horrifying results.

Although the Methodist most often imputed the physical agitations of the convert to the Holy Spirit, John Tottie, archdeacon of Worcester, writing to the clergy in the diocese of Worcester, was less certain. He asserted that the Holy Spirit normally operated in a less convulsive fashion: '... the Operations of the Spirit are not violent and tempestuous, agitating the whole human Frame and throwing it into convulsions, like the Dispossession of a Demoniac; nor are they ever attended with such Derelictions, Terrors, Despairings, Struggles and Pangs, as are almost equal to the Torments of Hell—but they are so gentle and peaceable in their Nature as they are in their Effects, and ... they cannot with certainty be discovered any other way than by the Fruits which they produce.' He later more strongly affirmed that the physical agitations present in such conversions were not necessary signs of a true conversion.[12]

Since the anti-Methodist was certain that the agitations of the Methodists were not caused by the Holy Spirit, he considered other possible causes for such convulsions.[13] Theophilus Evans attributed them to the boisterous delivery of the preacher. Another, perhaps half-facetiously, saw them resulting from the

[12] John Tottie, *Two Charges Delivered to the Clergy of the Diocese of Worcester* (Oxford, 1766), pp. 16, 21.
[13] Even Wesley was not always sure that the physical actions accompanying conversion were heaven-inspired. Sometimes he attributed them to the devil. Of Thomas Maxfield's conversion, he wrote: 'Except John Haydon [who had been converted a few days before], I never saw one so torn of the Evil One' (*Journal*, II.203).

SATIRE OF METHODIST CONVERTS AND CONVERSION

fermenting of enthusiastic yeast put into the heads of the converts.[14] But the most common allegation, non-satiric and satiric, was that the wild agitations of the Methodists were caused by drugs administered by the preachers. This was an attempt to explain an allegedly supernatural and almost miraculous occurrence by rational, natural causes. According to Ronald Knox, Bishop Lavington accused Wesley, who did prescribe physic for his fellow-Methodists, of dosing them with '... drugs to produce hysterical symptoms'.[15] The author of *Fanatical Conversion* attributed the conversions directly to the power of drugs:

> *Myst'ry's* the Trap; the Bait, a *lying Tongue*.
> But when to *Myst'ry* baneful *Physic's join'd*,
> The *Constitution's* weaken'd like the *Mind:*
> When Dupes by *Falsehood's* Doctrines are perplex'd,
> By pois'nous *Drugs* and *Priestcraft* doubly vex'd,
> Then who can wonder, when lewd *Philters* work,
> That *Miracles* beneath *Imposture* lurk?

The conversion experience among the eighteenth-century Methodists generally followed a pattern. The first step in that pattern, as has been indicated, is that the individual is first made aware that he is damned, that he is, in Methodist terms, a hopelessly lost sinner. This is the period of great despair, which is followed generally by a recognition that only Christ can atone for the individual's sins. After a more or less troubled period he is aware that he has been forgiven. The conversion process may be accompanied by wild, often involuntary, physical movements, cries, fallings to the ground, and other hysterical actions. The manifestations of a person in the throes of the New Birth were summarized by R. A. Knox: 'There is a cry, or a roar; usually (not always) the afflicted person drops to the ground; you can see that he or she is something in the position of the demoniac healed after the Transfiguration; Satan is letting his prey go,

---
[14] *Letter to the Rev. Mr M--re B--k-r*, p. 20.
[15] Knox, *Enthusiasm*, p. 425.

with the utmost reluctance. The bystanders fall to prayer; if there is no immediate deliverance the interrupter is carried out, and prayer goes on, often till late at night.'[16] The satiric descriptions of conversions employed generally the same manifestations.

While many of the satires simply ridiculed the physical peculiarities of such conversions, some attempted to satirize the whole pattern of conversion, or at least to present a whole conversion experience. Even these emphasize the physical agitations and loss of control of the convert, and they suggest that these physical phenomena were the principal signs of conversion. Thus the captain who desires to seduce Theodosia in *The Story of the Methodist-Lady* weeps, groans loudly, and laments bitterly in a feigned conversion which is accepted by the congregation as genuine. The author of *A Plain and Easy Road* depicted satirically the whole pattern of the conversion from the roaring and dropping down to the rhapsody of the delivered convert:

Making towards one of the doors, I espied an object screaming, as for a wager—her eyes were turn'd into her head, and I was told that they were engaged with her inward man. Her mouth was far advanced towards one of her ears; and she seem'd to me to have got so large a portion of the blast, that she was just ready to burst.—I thought the D—l was in her, or that she got the dry gripes;—but was told by a woman (who look'd like a whore) that she was got with child by what the teacher had said to her, and would, e'er long, bring forth. . . .

The patient laid, for some time, in one of the most indecent postures I ever saw; but no one was suffer'd to touch her, for fear of spoiling the operation.—Having at length, abundantly manur'd and plentifully shower'd, she opened her eyes, and spoke words, which I took to be crazy, incoherent stuff; but *now* am satisfied were revelations—the very words of truth and soberness.

This is generally characteristic of the descriptions of Methodist conversions, although Nathaniel Lancaster's saint describes in

[16] Ibid. p. 521.

the course of a sermon in slightly more theological terms the pattern of conversion which he expects to be followed:

> For till a Sinner fully is convinc'd,
> That Hell, his due desert, must be his Lot;
> A single Step he never will advance
> In that strait Path, which leads to Realms of Bliss
> But thus alarm'd, Damnation he expects.
> Then Groans and Sighs succeed, and then Despair—
> And next, dire Conflicts with Satanic Powers;
> Which Pray'r produce, and Pray'r produces Faith;
> And Faith, New Birth.—Thus Man is born again.

Yet even here as the saint and the devil strive—the one to cause and the other to prevent the New Birth from taking place—the labour is marked by 'Shrieks of Affright, and Wailings of Despair'. And one satire depicted the Methodists gyrating and tearing up the ground like maddened bulls.[17] A few anti-Methodists emphasized the emotional rather than the physical element of the conversion. Lackington's account of his own conversion is extremely restrained: 'At last, by singing and repeating enthusiastic amorous hymns, and presumptuously applying particular texts of scripture, I got my imagination to the proper pitch, was born again in an instant, became a very great favourite of heaven, and was so familiar with the Father, Son, and Holy Ghost, as any old woman in Mr Wesley's connection.'

Other satiric attacks simply ridiculed the physical manifestations of conversion without attempting to describe the conversion process. The writers of these were satisfied with depicting, in the words of Theophilus Evans, '... the shocking and horrible Things belonging to the History of this strange Sect, ... such as their Crying out, Screaming, Roaring, Groanings, Tremblings, Yellings, Convulsions, Swooning, Blasphemies, Curses, despairing Agonies, and Variety of Tortures in Body and Mind.'[18] These attacks graphically depicted converts in

[17] *Sketches for Tabernacle-Frames. A Poem* (London, 1778), pp. 26–7.
[18] *The History of Modern Enthusiasm*, p. 129.

convulsions, unable to control their bodily functions and babbling incoherently and rhapsodically.

The satirists busied themselves in depicting the results of the emotional upheaval called conversion. Although some satirists simply displayed the transformation of an innocent, pleasure-loving individual into a melancholy fanatic, the transformation of a Sir Toby Belch into a Malvolio, many depicted more serious results—suicide and often insanity. James Lackington said that he was '. . . metamorphosed into a dull, moping, psalm-singing fanatic, continually reprehending all about me for their harmless mirth and gaiety'. A Methodist seeking to enter the Elysian Fields is described as 'a strange Fellow, with a rueful Countenance, hollow Eyes, and all the Symptoms of Melancholy. . . .'[19] In the *Story of the Methodist-Lady* Sally, Theodosia's maid, regales her with the story of Dolly F - - h, who has hanged herself: '. . . they say it was by running after the Methodists that has brought her to this: For your Ladyship knows her Aunt was a great Follower of W - - d. . . .' According to the author of *A Plain and Easy Road*, the converts after they received the Eolian blast became preachers: '. . . the wholesome blast (after various struggles and grumblings, which ignorant men only take for the dry gripes or cholic, because of the patient's roaring and making ugly faces, and at last falling down into instructive and edifying fits) may—after a double or two about the bowels, stomach, head, &c.—come out in the shape and character of holding forth.' Thus the Methodist preachers inspire converts, who in turn become preachers to inspire more converts.

But much the most common result of the Methodist conversion depicted by the satirist was insanity. To the unsympathetic observer the Methodist, screaming and beating himself against the floor, must already have seemed insane. Here was reason deposed and mania crowned. Yet though the shock of conversion might produce insanity, as Lancaster ironically noted in

[19] *London Magazine* (1739), p. 451.

SATIRE OF METHODIST CONVERTS AND CONVERSION

Methodism Triumphant, 'It saves the soul; which Reason would destroy'. The depiction of insanity ranged from the mild statement that a Methodist's senses seemed to have left him to the blunt accusation that Bedlam was filled with Methodists.[20] Christopher Anstey, in *The New Bath Guide* (1794), has his young hero complain that his sister, who has been converted to Methodism, seems to have lost her senses. The mountebank doctor, who recognizes that his patients die as often as the Methodist preacher's become insane, suggests a compact between mountebanks: 'Let me add by way of hint as to *private* practice, that when I find my patients departing, I will turn them over to your care; converts are easily made in a dying hour, and a *will* may be drawn in your favour as *methodical* as you please. On the other hand, as one good turn deserves another, when you find the zeal of your patients begins to degenerate into *real* madness, send 'em to me to be purged, blistered, and dieted.'[21] Other satirists hinted that the number of inhabitants in Bedlam had increased because of the Methodists, but one author suggested boldly that the Methodists should build insane asylums rather than chapels: 'But if these gentlemen are determined to build, I would recommend to them the plan of a certain edifice founded by Dr *Swift*, which, if considerably augmented, may accommodate many of the religious mad in this country.[22]

The satirists thus depicted the Methodist convert as a gull or a hypocrite and the conversion itself as the apotheosis of irrationality. The Methodist preachers in the satires appealed to the illiterate, to the frightened, and to those of inferior mentality, notably women, to be born again. To make the rebirth of the convert as memorable as his original entry into the world, the preachers administered drugs which produced the hysterical symptoms of the New Birth. The convert, temporarily insane, powerless to control his bodily functions, flung himself on the

[20] See *A Letter from Mr Foote*, p. 30.
[21] *The Gentleman's Magazine* (1758), p. 101.
[22] *Letter to the Rev. Mr M--re B--k-r*, pp. 18–19.

ground, screamed obscenities, and fouled himself. After his entry into the ranks of the saved, if his sanity had not been permanently lost, he returned to his everyday life and habits—to cobble shoes and commit adultery. But if in saving his soul, he had lost his reason, he swelled the ranks of Bedlam or those of the inspired Methodist teachers.

CHAPTER SEVEN

Satire of John Wesley

TO AN EMPIRICAL age the life of a man is by that very fact one indication of the validity of his premises. Thus although the satirists of Methodism ridiculed many things about the movement, they inevitably had to strike at the heart of the matter—at the Methodist leaders themselves. The chief weapon at hand with which the satirists could attack the Methodists was personal satire. Thus whether they directly imitated Milton, Butler, Dryden, Pope, or Swift, the satirists tried to create new MacFlecknoes and new Sporuses—new prototypes of dullness and evil. The founders of Methodism, even though they might have lived devout lives, were as subject to vilification as the wildest of the French Prophets. The portraits of them which appear in the satires, although they are tinted with reality, are of course fictional creations. The John Wesley of the satires may bear as little resemblance to the actual as MacFlecknoe does to Thomas Shadwell or Sporus to Lord Hervey. Yet by creating a fictitious Wesley, the satirist, if we accept his professed motive, hoped to reveal the true Wesley whom the observer could not see for the outward man who moved behind a mask of religious hypocrisy. The actual motives of the satirist were probably many, but he must have struck at the Methodist movement—its beliefs and its practices—through the man. Momus, a satiric characterization of the dramatist Samuel Foote, justifies his use of the derisive term Dr Hunchback for the 'high priest of the conventicle': '... you must know that the whole success of our scheme depended upon it; for if I had not turned the ridicule against your person, the taste of the public is so gross, that I might have laughed alone at your opinions.'[1] By depicting the man as ridiculous or dangerous, the satirist revealed the absurdity and danger of the movement.

The satiric attacks on Wesley, although they were severe and at one point reached a crescendo of fury, were less scurrilous than those on the more untactful George Whitefield. Perhaps because Wesley's language and preaching were less florid and less enthusiastic, perhaps too because his Arminianism and his High Church leanings were less obnoxious to both orthodox and latitudinarian churchmen than Whitefield's Calvinism and easy mingling with Dissenters, Wesley, early in the rise of Methodism, seems to have suffered much less personal abuse than Whitefield, although of course the doctrines and practices of both were extensively attacked.

Although sporadic satiric outbursts flared up against Wesley throughout his life, the greatest flurry seems to have been caused by a political rather than a religious action, which won him many supporters as well as many enemies. That action was the publication in 1775 of a defence of the English Government's position on the American colonies, *A Calm Address to Our American Colonies*, a defence based on and in part copied from Dr Johnson's *Taxation No Tyranny*, published in the same year.[2] Within the next five years attack after attack accused Wesley of most vices, ridiculed his person and his beliefs, and denounced him and his source, Dr Johnson, as traitors to the English crown who sought to deny English rights to true-born Englishmen. In addition, the first half of the decade of the seventies was marred by a long and bitter warfare between the Wesleyans and the Calvinistic Methodists. It is thus within the next to the last decade of his life that the long-lived Wesley was most satirized.

In his personal appearance Wesley lacked the dramatic squint

[1] Charles Johnstone, *Chrysal or the Adventures of a Guinea*, ed. E. A. Baker (London, n.d.), p. 171.
[2] Shepherd asserts that the prestige of Wesley rose sharply in the seventies because of his support of the Government's position on the American Revolution. See *Methodism and the Literature of the Eighteenth Century*, p. 200.

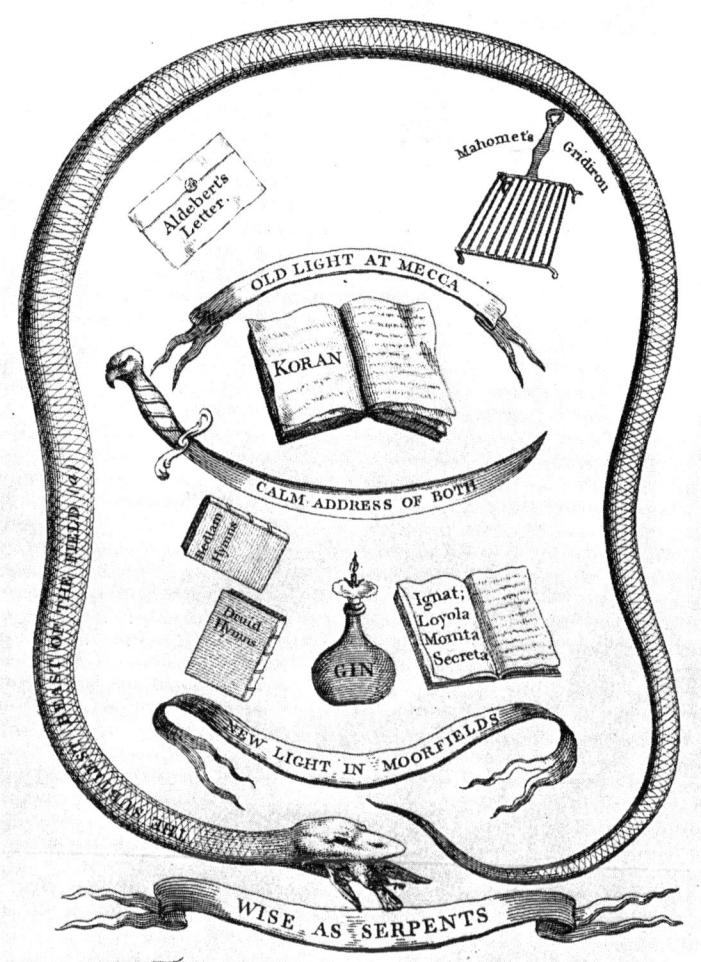

Frontispiece from *The Temple of Imposture, A Poem* (London, 1778) in which Mohamet intercedes for the Methodists with the goddess Furina.

of Whitefield, which gave him the popular sobriquet of Squintum, but the satirists nevertheless ridiculed his physical appearance or saw it as symbolic. The author of *The Temple of Imposture* used Wesley's short stature as symbolic of his vileness. Wesley approaches the throne of the Goddess Furina:

> A short, squat, *toothless Mufti*, mean and *proud*,
> *Stepp'd* forth a *Candidate;* of such a *Form*,
> As soon convinc'd me *Man* was but a *Worm*.³

The author of *Sketches for Tabernacle-Frames* in a similar manner saw symbolism, some of it ironic, in Wesley's features:

> His hoary *Head*, his penitential Face,
> His *flinty Front*, bespeak a *Babe of Grace*.
> His looks demure, his grave Deportment, Eyes
> *Half-clos'd*, denote him *pious, meek*, and *wise*.
> Those Eyes he'll open wide to give Offence,
> Steel'd with a most celestial *Impudence*. . . .

John Harman, who interpreted all things Methodist in the light of their supposed astrologically dominant planet, Saturn, simply endeavoured to demonstrate that John Wesley was saturnine: 'The planet Saturn for the generality, describes a person of a middling stature, but rather inclining to brevity; he being oriental, his complexion pale, swarthy, or muddy; his eyes little and black, looking downwards; black or sad hair; more black when in Virgo; there is a great likeness between the person of *John Wesley* and the description of this Planet.'

Since many of the satiric attacks on Wesley came in his old age, he is often depicted as a toothless, aged lecher. A long life has taught him guile. Reynardo [Wesley]⁴ preaches in *The Love-Feast:*

> *Reynardo* next (by *Mob* old *Cantwell* call'd),
> Much hurt to hear how wild *Romano* bawl'd,
> With *wheezing Whistle* whisks up his *whipt Cream;*

³ *The Temple of Imposture; a Poem* (London, 1778), p. 28.
⁴ 'Reynard', 'fox', 'wolf', and 'Cantwell' are all terms applied to Wesley.

Soft as the fleeting snow his *Whispers* seem.
Thus, like a *Zephyr*, late o'er *Bristol-Mead*,
He *calmly* wheez'd, and *felt* that *Wheeze* succeed. . . .[5]

He puts the infirmities of old age to advantage:

With Loss of *Teeth* he has not lost his *Wits*.
That *Accident* was fortunate, perhaps;
Old *Age*, grey *Hairs*, and *Mumbling*, are *fine Traps*.

Unlike Whitefield, Wesley was generally able to keep his private life from the speculations of the satirists; yet occasional references do appear. Wesley's departure from Georgia in 1737, leaving behind him an unsettled law suit brought by the husband of Sophia Hopkey, the girl with whom Wesley had considered marriage, and indictments brought by the magistrates, is alluded to in Lancaster's *Methodism Triumphant* when Satan tells the saint that it was he who enabled him to escape from Georgia, 'from the Pangs of persecuting Law'.[6] One satirist alleged that Wesley's near marriage to Grace Murray, a Methodist worker, which was prevented by Charles Wesley, did not take place because Wesley's desires were sated.[7] Finally one satirist explained Wesley's separation from his wife, the former Mrs Molly Vazeille, who turned over to her husband's enemies mutilated versions of his letters, to Wesley's preference for new and younger companions:

At *sixty-three* could such *Perfection burn?*
No *Victim* but in *Teens* then serve your Turn,
Till on a Widow Int'rest made you fix,
Faithless alike in *Love* and *Politics?*

[5] 'Romano' is the Reverend William Romaine, a Calvinistic Methodist. After 1775 the adjective 'calm' and the adverb 'calmly' were used in every possible situation to describe Wesley or his actions.

[6] The Georgia episode is discussed in detail in Tyerman's *Life of Wesley*, I.153-64.

[7] See *Voltaire's Ghost to the Apostle of the Sinless Foundery: a Familiar Epistle from the Shades* (London, 1779), p. 22. Accounts of the Grace Murray episode and his marriage are treated in most biographies of Wesley, but see particularly Chapters 21 and 22 of Arnold Lunn's *John Wesley* (New York, 1929).

SATIRE OF JOHN WESLEY

> Stronger than *Marriage-Vows* rank Lust inclin'd
> *Sinless Perfection* soon to change its Mind;
> The *Wife* grew stale—you found *some Converts* kind.[8]

One strategy of the satirists of Methodism was to attribute an event to a cause other than the one assigned by the Methodists. Thus the agitation of the converts, ostensibly caused by the operation of the Holy Spirit, actually resulted from drugs administered by the preachers. In much the same way, the satirists attributed Wesley's religious inspiration to several sources; the attacks of course were primarily personal and aimed at Wesley himself. The most conventional attribution of the inspiration is to Satan, although he is often forced to share the honour with such goddesses as Phantasia and Furina, the last of which is apparently intended as a personification of confusion and chaos. In Lancaster's *Methodism Triumphant* after the divine Phantasia has hailed Wesley as 'My Pride—my Glory—and my high Delight!' and has urged him to challenge Satan to single combat, Satan reveals to Wesley that his preaching skill is fiendishly inspired, that his inspiration is infernal rather than heavenly:

> That Flow of Words, which is thy daily boast,
> Was my free gift: and all those floods of Grace,
> Not from the Skies, but from the Stygian Gulph,
> Were pour'd into thy breast.—I bade them take
> Delusive Forms of Gospel Piety.
> Thy Dreams, thy Visions, thy Fanatic Zeal,
> Boasted Perfection, Sanctimonious Pride,
> And thy fond Thirst for Glory, from me rose. . . .

Then like a wrathful God hurling thunder bolts at a rebellious angel, Satan accuses Wesley of treachery:

> In this high Emprise
> Thee I selected for my Substitute,

---

[8] *Perfection*, p. 15.

> Vicegerent in this Globe, to take my Seat;
> And act, for me, thy delegated Part.
> But thou art false, a Traitor to thy King!

When the saint is victorious, Phantasia has triumphed. But the saint pulls off the devil's tail and hangs it above his chapel, where it remains as an ironic symbol of Satanic influence:

> There must it hang, till Time shall be no more.
> There hang, a Trophy of victorious Faith,
> And surest Proof, that METHODISM springs,
> With all her Tenets, from an Heav'nly Source.

In *The Temple of Imposture*, Mahomet, as intent on seeing that his disciple Wesley is treated properly as Dryden's Flecknoe on determining the succession to the throne of Dullness, prays to the goddess Furina:

> Aid *W - - y's* Arts, as once you prospered mine,
> And make his *Phrenzies* pass for *Calls divine*.

The goddess hears his prayer and promises that Wesley, by virtue of his great enthusiasm and knavery, will become her heir:

> For *true Ambition* I reserve *one Post*,
> In which the greatest *Knave* shall flourish most.
> To him alone shall this Department fall
> Who from his *Feelings thinks he has a Call*.
> Ev'n *We Ourselves* will crown his pious Care,
> And of our well-fix'd Throne adopt him *Heir*.
> *Fraud* shall afford him a continual Feast,
> Whilst Virtue starves; and he shall be our Priest.

In their main outlines Wesley's theological beliefs, though they may have softened a little as he aged, did not change after his acceptance of Arminianism and salvation by faith. Yet his expression of them did change as he attempted to mollify the Calvinists or decided to take a stand against them. These changes, insignificant though they may be, caused the satirists to depict Wesley as a Protean figure, changing his views as the situation demanded. The attacks are upon Wesley rather than his views. For example, the author of *Methodism and Popery Dissected and Compared* wrote indignantly:

Read his writings as a Divine, and I am positive any Gentleman acquainted with Religious Controversy would, with the SORBONNE, declare him a JESUIT, a RANK CATHOLICK. Peruse his answer to *Doctor Warburton,* you would pronounce him a *Serjeant at Law.* Hear him preach one day at the Foundery, and you would swear he was a good *Actor.* Take a turn to the Seven-Dials the next morning, and ten to one (if the weather changed) but Implicit Faith, the *doctrine of the Mother-Church* [perhaps Roman Catholic] is his Theme; and in the evening an Anabaptist. Every Sunday he is a Lutheran; the following day he sides with *mad* JACK CALVIN; and if the weather proves mild (by his mental Barometer) on Tuesday, he cannot tell *what Religion* he is of himself, unless he is destined to hold forth: and then, as he has all Religions by him, he takes no care, but gives his Congregation what first comes uppermost. . . .[9]

Many of the attacks on Wesley's religious beliefs came from the Calvinist Methodists, who after the controversial Methodist Conference of 1770 were no longer to be mollified.[10]

The satirists were, of course, delighted by this evidence of disharmony among the saints. Although Wesley was obviously not the only controversialist ridiculed, many satirists were pleased to depict him as the serpent in the Methodist Paradise. An interview between Wesley and the devil alleged that Wesley stirred up the Calvinist controversy out of boredom.[11] The author of *A Plain and Easy Road* asserted that Wesley opened a new turnpike after he began to find fault with the one set up by Mr Orator—[Whitefield]. Ironically the Methodist apologist accuses Wesley of heresy and schism:

[9] *Methodism and Popery Dissected and Compared* (London, 1779), pp. 55–6.
[10] See particularly *A Conversation between Richard Hill, Esq.; the Rev. Mr Madan, and the Superior of a Convent of English Benedictine Monks at Paris* (London, 1772), p. 13.
[11] *The Gospel Magazine,* IV (1777), p. 330.

These men [a group instructed by the orator] (to their shame be it spoken) began to wax wanton, and most ungratefully to find many faults with his road. One of them [Wesley] advanced that it did not lead to bliss in a streight line enough; and therefore it was necessary that an alteration should be made. What does he do them—but *heretically* and *schismatically* strikes out a bye-road, and sets up a turnpike for himself;—makes proclamation, That *his* was the safer and more *direct* way than Mr ——'s; he threatens also, that those who would not immediately leave the other tract, and come into his, should be d—n'd; and thus he drew away many customers from dear Mr Orator ——.

Closely related to the attack upon the shifts in Wesley's religious views was his assumption of more than one profession. Probably he would have been able to continue all his many activities as priest, religious controversialist, and even political writer without his professional qualifications being questioned, had he not published in 1747 *Primitive Physick; or an Easy and Natural Method of Curing Most Diseases* and had he not dispensed remedies to his Methodists. His assumption of the role of physician made it easy for the satirists to brand him as a quack in medicine, religion, and politics. As has been noticed, the satirists were quick to see a connection between the violent emotional behaviour of the Methodists and the fact that their leader dispensed medical advice.

Wesley's quackery is emphasized in a lengthy portrayal in *Sketches for Tabernacle-Frames*. He is as qualified for all three of his occupations as for one:

> He (that his ready Bow may never lack
> A String) is *Preacher*, *Pamphleteer*, and *Quack*.
> Equally form'd for each Department, all
> He fills alike to each he has a *Call*.
> *Toothless*, yet to the toughest *Text's* he's just;
> A knotty Point he'll mumble like a Crust;
> And tho' you cannot edify one Letter,
> Yet few can *whistle* off rank Nonsense better.

Then, as an Author, ...
He'll prove that *white* is black, or *black* is white;
And, (vice versa,) cross but his Positions,
He'll baffle, and outlie, most *Politicians*.

Similarly, Murcia, in *The Love-Feast*, damns Reynardo [Wesley] with faint praise as skilfully as Atticus might have done:

At thy thrice-hallow'd Birth *Apollo* smil'd,
And with his *choicest Arts* endu'd *his Child*.
In *Physic* He design'd Thee to be great;
In *Poetry* He bid Thee rival *Tate;*
For *pious Hymns* thy Genius equals *Quarles*,
Seraphic Partner of thy Brother Ch - - les.

Other satirists were content to ridicule Wesley's medical activity and lewdly to attribute other motives to his practice than the desire to cure. The author of *Fanatical Conversion* suggested that the answer to the question of why Wesley's congregations experienced such spasms was a simple one but that their souls really suffered more than their bodies:

I answer,—'*John's* Priest, Wizard, and Physician:
Starv'd *Bodies* with apt *Nostrums* he controuls,
And with worse Physic stupefies their Souls.'

The Methodist preachers, he continued, had become physicians of body and soul:

Thus, at cheap Rates, *Health* and *Salvation's* sure;
Thus *Christ's Apostles* now *absolve* and *cure*,
With Preaching, Pray'r, *Drugs Primitive* and Psalm
But most of all with true *Perfection's Balm*.

No part of Wesley's career was more attacked than his publishing, and no single publication was attacked more severely than *A Calm Address*, published late in his career. Works published earlier, principally his *Journals*, portions of which had been published as early as 1739,[12] were occasionally satirized. By 1767 Lancaster in *Methodism Triumphant* was ridiculing the size of the *Journals*. His saint first uses his *Journals* as a shield, but later defeats Satan by the sheer weight of them. After a prayer that celestial powers will aid him so that he may triumph, 'And all Mankind may Methodists commence', the enthusiastic David, given supernatural strength, hurls the weapon:

> —and thrice his massive Journals shook—
> Thrice swung them round—then hurl'd them up aloft:—
> When by celestial vehemence impell'd,
> High and more high they flew, roaring as fierce
> As fiercest Whirlwinds in their airy Flight.

One phrase from the *Journals*, the famous and well-turned affirmation by Wesley that the whole world was his parish, was singled out for satire. One author wrote of a letter by Wesley to the *Morning Post* concerning the publication of an edition of Voltaire: 'What a pious, primitive *oecumenical* Concern is here displayed for the darling Interests of *Methodism*; the *only true Old Christianity*. . . .' He justified the use of *oecumenical* 'Because the *whole World* is a *Methodist-Preacher's* Parish. . . .'[13] The author of *Fanatical Conversion* assigned Wesley to be, '*John*, Diocesan of all *Moorfields*', but recognized in a note: 'But a scanty District for an itinerant Apostle, who boasts that *the whole World is his Parish*. . . .' Although Wesley's hymns and particularly his abridgement, with its Calvinism heightened, of Augustus Toplady's translation of Zanchius, drew some attacks, other satiric references to Wesleyan publications, except for *A Calm Address*, are infrequent.[14]

The appearance in 1775 of Wesley's *Calm Address*, marking

[12] This date is suggested by Nehemiah Curnock in Wesley, *Journal*, I, Preface, vii.
[13] The phrase is used in a letter to James Hervey, but Wesley includes portions of the letter in his *Journal* entry for 11th June 1739. *Journal*, II.218. *Voltaire's Ghost to the Apostle of the Sinless Foundery*, p. vi.
[14] See Toplady, V.319, and *A Review of All the Doctrines Taught by the Rev. Mr John Wesley*, p. 31.

a change from Wesley's earlier sympathy with the American colonists, unleashed a pack of satiric assaults. The tract, abridged from Dr Johnson's *Taxation No Tyranny*, seemed to have been approved of by Johnson, according to Herbert, although the original source was not indicated on the title page or in the pamphlet.[15] Johnson himself later was extremely flattering. He wrote Wesley in 1776: 'I have thanks... to return you for the addition of your important suffrage to my argument on the American question. To have gained such a mind as yours, may justly confirm me in my own opinion. What effect my paper has had upon the publick, I know not; but I have no reason to be discouraged. The Lecturer was surely in the right, who, though he saw his audience slinking away, refused to quit the Chair, while Plato staid.'[16] The Government reaction was highly favourable. According to Tyerman, the Government ordered copies of the pamphlet distributed at the doors of all metropolitan churches.[17] The reaction expressed in the satires was slightly less enthusiastic.

The kind of treatment that Wesley received is indicated in the title of one of the satires which puns upon the title of Wesley's pamphlet: *Perfection. A Poetical Epistle. Calmly Addressed to the Greatest Hypocrite in England*. According to Herbert, Wesley was charged by his opponents with plagiarism, inflaming of the mind of the public, being a turncoat since he had earlier espoused the American position, and being ambitious for preferment in the Church.[18] Certainly the satires castigated

---

[15] Herbert, *John Wesley as Editor and Author*, p. 108. Tyerman, *Life of Wesley*, III.186. Although Boswell does not indicate Johnson's opinion of the pamphlet, Boswell's note on Johnson's statement that Wesley, in contrast to Whitefield, thought only of religion indicates clearly that Boswell disapproved of the pamphlet. *Journal of a Tour to the Hebrides*, in Boswell's *Life of Johnson*, V.35–6.
[16] *The Letters of Samuel Johnson*, collected and edited by R. W. Chapman (Oxford, 1952), II.101.
[17] Tyerman, *Life of Wesley*, II.191.
[18] Herbert, *John Wesley as Editor and Author*, p. 108. Some alleged that Wesley's motive in publishing *A Calm Address* was a desire for a bishopric, and these allegations will be considered in the examination of the satire of Wesley's ambitions.

Wesley unmercifully for plagiarism, since Wesley's pamphlet, an obvious abridgement of *Taxation No Tyranny*, did not mention Johnson's and was presumably to be read as an original composition. An anonymous satirist in *The Gospel Magazine* accused Wesley directly of plagiarism:

> Though, ev'ry-body knows, he took
> His Calm Address, from JOHNSON's book!
> And loudly then he cry'd ' 'Tis Mine.'[19]

Other satirists, continuing to use the charge of plagiarism, ridiculed the transformation of an eighteen-penny pamphlet into a two-penny one. Wesley is a pirate come as if from Heaven 'Charg'd with a *two-penny Address*'. Toplady stigmatized Wesley as 'a low and puny tadpole in divinity', as 'a methodist weather-cock' who 'saluted the public with a two-penny paper (extracted by whole paragraphs together from the aforesaid doctor), ycleped, A Calm Address to our American Colonies'.[20]

The satiric accusations that Wesley sought to inflame the public mind played on the title of the pamphlet. The pamphlet was '*Calm* only in the Title-Page'.[21] The author of *Perfection* accused Wesley of massacre:

> But, above all, thou Friend to *Public Good!*
> Stir up *Revenge* to shed a *Nation's Blood;*
> Wing *Desolation*, aggravate *Distress*,
> Turn those to *Tyrants* who should live to *bless*,
> And *massacre* Mankind with CALM ADDRESS.

Wesley had published this inflammatory pamphlet 'To gain the *Mob, that Beast with many Heads*'.[22] The author of *The Fanatic Saints* depicted Wesley as a totalitarian spiritual

---

[19] *The Gospel Magazine*, IV (1777), p. 226.
[20] See *Voltaire's Ghost to the Apostle of the Sinless Foundery*, p. 44, and Toplady, *Works*, V.442.
[21] *Voltaire's Ghost to the Apostle of the Sinless Foundery*, p. 45.
[22] *Sketches for Tabernacle-Frames*, p. 20.

guide who used his religious influence to win others to his evil:

> That *Freemen* dare revolt this *Saint* complains;
> Yet like a *Tyrant* o'er Mens *Souls* he *reigns*,
> Makes *Piety* a *Bawd* to aid his Work,
> Outlies *Sam. J - - s - n*, and out-whores a Turk.

The most elaborate satiric attack on the *Calm Address* came in a twenty-page pamphlet written by Patrick Bull (probably a pseudonym) which alleged, referring to the supposed credulity of both Wesley and Johnson about ghosts, that both pamphlets had been written by the ghost of Father Petre, whom the advertisement identified as the Jesuit '... who endeavoured to establish Popery and Despotism in the Reign of *James* the Second...'.[23] The author begins by pointing out that Wesley could not be the author of the pamphlet because his views are entirely opposed to those of *A Calm Address*. He resolved the apparent paradox by explaining that a ghost must have written it: 'True, a ghost it was, but his ghost it could not be; for though he were even politically, morally, and spiritually dead, it is certain that he is not naturally so, and I will prove, from the doctrines of the pamphlet, that it was the ghost of a Jesuit....' The author then visits Dr Johnson, who agrees that Wesley could not have written it and ironically asserts that the same spirit has written a recent pamphlet called *Taxation No Tyranny:*

> The Doctor, who, as he was born with a *caul over his face*, is consequently a cunning man, and has the gift of discerning spirits, agreed entirely with me in sentiment; adding, at the same time, that he knew the Spirit who was the *real* author of them as well as he knew *himself*, and that the same spirit had lately published a famous pamphlet, entitled *Taxation no Tyranny*, of which the *Calm Address* was only an abstract, divested of all the bombast of eloquence, to adapt it to the understanding of common readers, that the poison might spread universally.

Finally the author attempted to demonstrate, perhaps only half

[23] Patrick Bull, *A Wolf in Sheep's Cloathing: or, An Old Jesuit Unmasked* (Dublin printed, London reprinted [1775]), p. [2].

ironically, that the pamphlet was treasonable: 'I lay down these three propositions: First, that the arguments are sophistical or jesuitical, which are synonimous terms. Secondly, that they are injurious to his Majesty, because calculated to prove him an absolute monarch. And, thirdly, that they are written in favour of his Royal Highness *Prince Charles*, since they prove that the present family has no right to the crown.'

One of the satiric charges faced by Wesley in his old age was that he was ambitious, specifically that he desired a bishopric, although some of the satirists alleged simply that he sought preferment in the Church. Some of the general accusations that Wesley desired a bishopric grew out of the publication of *A Calm Address* since expediency provided an easy explanation of the change in Wesley's political views. Toplady alleged that Vulposo [Wesley] plundered Johnson's pamphlet in the hope of getting a bishopric. Patrick Bull, continuing his fiction that a Jesuit ghost wrote the pamphlet, asserted that Wesley really deserved a bishopric but that the author of the pamphlet deserved hanging: 'It has been said, that Mr Wesley has solicited to be made bishop of Quebec, that he may convert the papists from their errors, which preferment he undoubtedly deserves; whereas whoever dares to maintain the *jacobitical doctrines* contained in the *Calm Address*, instead of *lawn sleeves* should be presented with a *hempen* neckcloth, and, instead of a mitre, his head should be adorned with a white nightcap which in justice ought to be drawn over his eyes.'

The chorus of accusations that Wesley was ambitious swelled after 1763, when Erasmus, the Bishop of Arcadia, a bishop of the Greek Orthodox Church, ordained six Methodist laymen. It was rumoured that Wesley had requested consecration by him but had been refused. Erasmus's own credentials, according to Elliott-Binns, were questionable, but Tyerman asserted that Wesley had verified them, at least to his own satisfaction. The ordination of one of the laymen at least, according to Tyerman, was urged by Wesley, but at any rate all were expelled shortly from the Methodist society.[24] The allegation that Wesley himself sought consecration, apparently begun in *Lloyd's Morning Post* and continued by Toplady, is more questionable; indeed, it seems to have had no foundation.[25] Whether the accusation was true or not, the satires thereafter bristled with references to Erasmus. The author of *Fanatical Conversion* accused Wesley of being ambitious and asked: 'Else why were Forty Guineas offered to *Erasmus*, a mock Bishop of Acadia; to make a certain *Foundery Apostle* a Bishop?' The author of *Voltaire's Ghost* ridiculed the qualifications of both Erasmus and Wesley: 'Alas! alas! that a *mock Bishop* should have refused to *beatify* a *mock Apostle!*—an *Apostle* revered for his conspicuous *Piety* in *Georgia, Ireland, Scotland, England, Hernhuth,* and—*Moorfields.*'[26] But Venus, in *The Love-Feast*, consoles Wesley for his failure to attain his desire and awards him a diocese in which Bedlam might well be his episcopal seat:

> Churlish *Erasmus* gave You *no* Degree;
> That *Consecration* now receive from *Me:*
> To *Me* the richest Crops *thy Doctrine* yields;
> *Thine* be the *Diocese* of all *Moorfields.*

Finally the anti-Methodist satirists indulged in routine name-calling which bore little direct relationship to Wesley personally. He was called a Papist, a deceiver, a liar, and a lecher. He drew his income from his converts—his daws, cuckoos, and boobies. The author of *Perfection* depicted Wesley's gulls literally:

> Behold! from East and West, and North and South,
> *Gulls* drop their *Scraps* in *Cantwell's* toothless Mouth:
> To feed their *Prophet*, plunder all the Land,
> And fly to hear what none can understand. . . .

[24] Elliott-Binns, *The Early Evangelicals*, p. 222. Tyerman, *Life of Wesley*, II.486. Umphrey Lee refers to Erasmus as a bishop of the Greek Orthodox Church (see *The Lord's Horseman* [New York, 1954], p. 201).
[25] See Tyerman, *Life of Wesley*, II.486-7, and Lee, *The Lord's Horseman*, p. 201.
[26] *Voltaire's Ghost to the Apostle of the Sinless Foundery*, p. vi. Herrnhut was the Moravian settlement in Germany visited by Wesley.

Wesley is able to depict the deformity of Sin vividly because he has known her well.[27] But these accusations play no distinctive part in the satire of Wesley.

The John Wesley created in the satires is, from the satirists' point of view, the real John Wesley unmasked. This is the John Wesley whom the satirists wished the public to see. The pious Anglican priest who normally preached three times a day and who felt compelled to make known his changed views on the American colonies has his hypocrisy stripped away in the satires. He stands, or rather squats, displayed in all his ridiculousness or his vileness, depending on the satiric description. The fictional John Wesley is an aged lecher who is dominated by his physical appetites or by his self-interest. Though toothless and white haired, he doses his female converts with aphrodisiacs to make their moral conversion easier; Proteus-like he makes his views on the American colonies agree with those of the Government in the hope of being made a bishop. Yet he is also Cantwell, Reynard, the fox, the wolf in sheep's clothing, the man innately evil who is dominated by his diabolic inspiration and who is motivated by a Satanic desire to destroy mankind. The Wesley of the satires, although he is occasionally depicted as the fool in the midst of his ridiculousness, is more often a monster shaped like a man in the midst of his evil.

[27] *Methodism Triumphant*, p. 33.

CHAPTER EIGHT

Satire of George Whitefield

DESPITE THEIR severe ridicule of John Wesley the eighteenth-century satirists of Methodism reserved their most scathing personal attacks for Wesley's flamboyant fellow-evangelist, George Whitefield. Wesley, though he held such dangerously antinomian doctrines as salvation by faith and though he had embarked upon a career of field preaching and itineration, was by nature a conservative, and his general respectability was recognized, to some extent, even by his adversaries. Whitefield, on the other hand, apparently aroused indignation and ridicule by his simplest actions.

While the flood of attacks on Wesley came after the publication of *A Calm Address* in 1775, no such single period or incident marks the peak of the satire of Whitefield. The attacks began soon after his ordination to the diaconate in 1736 and continued even after his death in 1770. Probably, however, two periods represent the height of the anti-Whitefield attacks, 1738–42 and 1760–2. At the beginning of Whitefield's successful career in 1738 he found churches open to him and overflowing for him.[1] Yet in the same year soon after his return from his first visit to Georgia the mounting opposition barred him from preaching in most churches. Also in 1738 he had published his *Journals of a Voyage from London to Gibraltar, and from Gibraltar to Savannah*,[2] an action for which he was severely censured. The fact that of 200 anti-Methodist publications, not simply satires, issued during 1739 and 1740, 154 were aimed at

[1] Townsend, *et al., A New History* I.261.
[2] A. D. Belden, p. 52. Belden asserts that the publication was without Whitefield's knowledge; but see Lam and Smith, 'Two Rival Editions of George Whitefield's *Journal*,' *SP* (1944), p. 93.

Whitefield indicates the extent of the attacks against him.[3] The flurry of the second period, 1760-2, was probably inspired by Samuel Foote's 'take-off' of Whitefield in *The Minor*. The satiric portrait of Dr Squintum, as Whitefield was characterized in the play, was copied, attacked, defended, and simply commented upon. This single characterization of Whitefield in fact created a sizable body of publications.

The satiric attacks on Whitefield, though they were in general more severe than those on Wesley and indeed occasionally scurrilous, ranged from the mild *A Plain Address to the Followers and Favourers of the Methodists*, a pious attempt to convince the Methodists that the conduct of Whitefield was irregular,[4] to the obscenities of *The Expounder Expounded*.[5] As in the attacks on Wesley, the anti-Methodists sought to create a fictional Whitefield who would be associated with the actual one and the movement he represented. Many of the satirists, however, saw Whitefield as an absurd, pompous fraud whose pretensions should be punctured. Far more than for Wesley, the satirists concentrated on Whitefield's physical appearance, incidents from his personal life, and personal characteristics.

An obvious characteristic of Whitefield's physical appearance was a slight deformity: a squint in his left eye caused by the neglect of a nurse when, as a child, he had had the measles.[6] The satirists used the squint as the chief physical characteristic of the Whitefield they created. Probably originated by Samuel Foote in *The Minor*, the term *Dr Squintum* became the most popular satiric identification of Whitefield,[7] and the character

[3] C. Harold King, 'God's Dramatist', *Studies in Speech and Drama* . . ., p. 369.
[4] Although the work, published in London, is not dated, its contents make it seem early, perhaps 1738 or 1739.
[5] This pamphlet was apparently extremely popular, since two other pamphlets are identical to *Expounder* except for the title pages. See *Genuine and Secret Memoirs Relating to the Life and Adventures of That Arch Methodist, Mr G. W--fi--d* (Oxford, 1742) and *The Methodists Dissected* (Oxford, n.d.).
[6] A. D. Belden, *George Whitefield: The Awakener*, p. 28.
[7] According to the anonymous *An Additional Scene to the Comedy of The Minor* (London, 1761), Foote stole the idea for his play from Joseph Reed's *The Register-Office*, published in 1761.

was used as the satiric hero of Israel Pottinger's *The Methodist* and the anonymous *The Spiritual Minor* and as a leading character in a number of satires growing out of the Foote portrayal.

The squint itself was given considerable symbolic importance. Although Dr Squintum never appears in *The Minor*, the readiness with which Mrs Cole, a procuress, cites him as the reconciler of her two worlds of bawdry and religious devotion suggests that the squint was a winking at the demands of orthodox religious faith. Peter Paragraph, perhaps a pseudonym for Foote himself,[8] suggested in 1767 that it was a mark, like that of Cain, placed as a warning by God:

'Tis no where in the Scripture hinted,
That an Apostle ever squinted;
But power to them and Grace was given,
To look directly up to Heaven; . . .
Some folks may think this maxim's odd;
But mark the Man that's mark'd by God.[9]

In Evan Lloyd's *The Methodist* Satan twists the hero's eyes grotesquely askew as a mark of his obedience to Satan. The fiend, recognizing the appropriateness of the mark, tells his new servant that it is symbolic of his hypocrisy, parallel to the difference between what he does and what he says. The author of a commentary upon Whitefield's autobiography assumed that the devil, trying Whitefield, actually bound him upon a wheel, where the squint was effected accidentally: 'It was in one of these *Searcings* that Mr *W - - d* unhappily turning upon his Face, received that Detriment in his Eyes, from the raking of a rusty Nail, which has made a *Blinkard* of him ever since;

[8] Peter Paragraph first appeared as a 'take-off' of the Dublin printer George Faulkner in Foote's *The Orators*, produced at the Haymarket in 1762. In the play Paragraph is identified by one of the on-stage audience as Foote himself.
[9] Peter Paragraph, *The Methodist and Mimick* (2nd edn, London, 1767), p. 16.

and takes off considerably from that *Grace* and *Comeliness*, which otherwise flows round his Person.'[10] Other satirists, using the squint basically as a symbol of hypocrisy, saw it as indicative of Whitefield's attraction to the carnal while he looked up at the spiritual. Thus the author of *The Celebrated Lecture on Heads* describes one of the righteous overmuch: 'With one eye he looks up to Heaven, to make his congregation think he is devout, that's his spiritual eye; and with the other eye he looks down to see what he can get; and that's his carnal eye....'[11]

By publishing in 1740 an injudicious autobiography, *An Account of God's Dealings with the Reverend Mr George Whitefield*, the evangelist bared many details of his early life and furnished his satirists with wide targets for their barbs.

The author of *The Expounder Expounded* employed Whitefield's own technique of seeing great significance in trivial incidents. Thus the satirist sought prenatal influences which would serve as omens of Whitefield's future greatness. He asserted that Mrs Whitefield, at the time of George Whitefield's birth, suffered from colic and had a number of carminatives administered. Then the satirist gravely wrote: 'THE Nature of this Gentlewoman's Disorder, namely, *Wind*, was I affirm it, a double Emblem, ... both of the Doctrines which her Son was to deliver, and the Place they were to be delivered in; and we have accordingly beheld him upon the Hills and the House-tops, mounted up upon his aerial Throne, with Wings displayed like another Aeolus, belching out his divine Vapours to the Multitude, to the great Ease of himself, and Emolument of his Auditors.'

Whitefield's birth in the Bell Inn, Gloucester, an inn owned by his father, a wine merchant, was extensively commented

---

[10] R--ph J-ps-n, *The Expounder Expounded* (London, 1740), p. 53.
[11] [George Alexander Stevens] *The Celebrated Lecture on Heads* (London, 1765), p. 19. Although Whitefield is not named, the speaker is identified by a squint and as 'one of the righteous overmuch', a reference to a series of sermons preached by Dr Joseph Trapp, rector of Harlington in Sussex, to a congregation including Whitefield and published in 1739 as *The Nature, Folly, Sin, and Danger of Being Righteous Overmuch*.

upon. The same satirist suggested ironically that the name of the inn was significant: '. . . the Bell is certainly a Symbol of Renown, and is significative of much Noise and Rumour in the World: This may very naturally be applied to the person of Mr *W - - - d*, whose Fame is so happily inlarged and dilated thro' either Hemisphere.' When Tom Jones stopped at the Bell Inn some years later, Fielding wrote of it: 'The master of it is brother to the great preacher Whitefield; but is absolutely untainted with the pernicious principles of Methodism, or of any other heretical sect.'[12] Even later when the hero of *The Spiritual Quixote*, Geoffrey Wildgoose, and his Sancho, Jeremiah Tugwell, stop at the Bell in order to visit the place where their spiritual master was born, they are turned away by Mrs Whitefield, George Whitefield's sister-in-law, who complains that everyone wants to stop because Tom Jones once spent the night there. The great master, ironically, has been forgotten in the place of his birth.

One of the things which most delighted the satirists was an admission in the *Account of God's Dealings* of an 'abominable secret sin' of Whitefield's adolescence.[13] The recording of the commission of such a sin, so thinly veiled, permitted and even encouraged considerable speculation as to its exact nature. John Harman, working on a supposed astrological basis, suggested that the sin was sodomy. But the author of *The Expounder Expounded* dismissed this as well as adultery and incest. He then developed slowly and obscenely an elaborate revelation of the sin: 'Those who come nearest to the Mark, assert, That the Text would imply some very odd Intercourse of a *venerous* Nature, which passed between my Author and his *good* Friend the *Devil* and insinuate, that *Satan* might possibly become a *Succubus* for the Satisfaction of his *Particular:* But I answer, that there is more Reason to suppose his Favours to be of the *Incubus* Kind, since, in their Bed-Correspondence, Mr *W - - d*

[12] Henry Fielding, *The History of Tom Jones, a Foundling* (New York, 1943), p. 361.
[13] The work is reprinted in Tyerman's *Life of Whitefield* (see I.7).

tells us . . . that the *Devil* was always uppermost.'¹⁴ The satirist suggested finally that Whitefield's secret sin was '. . . the very same for which Heaven, taking *Tamar's* Part, destroyed the invidious and disappointing Onan.'

Other satirists ridiculed the extent to which Whitefield at Oxford in his zeal carried his abstinence and mortification. Not only did he observe the fasts of the Church rigorously but also, in his words: '. . . I began to leave off eating fruits and such like, and gave the money I usually spent in that way to the poor. Afterwards I always chose the worst sort of food, though my place furnished me with variety. I fasted twice a week. My apparel was mean. I thought it unbecoming for a penitent to have his hair powdered. I wore woollen gloves, a patched gown and dirty shoes, and therefore looked upon myself as very humble.'¹⁵ This exaggerated abstemiousness was depicted in the satires as a refraining even from lawful joys. A daemon in *Sketches for Tabernacle-Frames* tells the Methodist converts that a renunciation of life's comforts opens the way to salvation:

> *One Care* alone your Names *above* enrols;
> Encas'd in *Dirt*, the purer dwell your *Souls;*
> To Heav'n thro' *Filth* the *perfect Christian* steers;
> *Slovens* and *Sluts* are Christ's head-*Volunteers*.

The author attributed this 'healthy Doctrine' to Whitefield.

The personal revelations which Whitefield had made in these early publications, the *Journals* and the *Account of God's Dealings*, had drawn considerable fire, but some anti-Methodists attacked the publications themselves. As literary or even spiritual works they were found sadly wanting. Joseph Trapp, one of Whitefield's earliest antagonists, wearily characterized the

---

[14] The implication of homosexuality, which the satirist immediately corrects, may have arisen from his imitation of Pope's 'A Letter to a Noble Lord'. See *The Works of Alexander Pope*, ed. Whitwell Elwin and William John Courthope (London, 1889), V. 430.
[15] Cited in A. D. Belden, *George Whitefield: The Awakener*, p. 21.

Journal as 'that Rhapsody of Madness, Spiritual Pride, and little less than Blasphemy, if not quite so; which this *Field-Preacher* calls his *Journal* . . .'.[16] When the lapdog Pompey, the picaresque hero of Coventry's *Pompey the Little* defecated upon a copy of Whitefield's *Journal*, Coventry suggested that the dog might have chosen this action to indicate his opinion of the book. One satirist suggested that *An Account of God's Dealings* should be entitled *A Short Account of the Devil's Dealings with the Reverend Mr G - - e W - - d;* the Bishop of Exeter stigmatized the work as 'a perfect Jakes of Uncleanness'.[17] Shamela's master, in Fielding's novel, discovers her reading the *Dealings* and accuses her of reading the Earl of Rochester's poems, a comparison which reveals the kind of book the *Dealings* was satirically reputed to be.[18]

Whitefield's oratory and his language were extensively satirized. His deeply moving and powerful voice and his dramatic gestures made him a famous orator. Lackington, who heard Whitefield preach about 1770 at the Tabernacle, wrote of the experience: '. . . of all the preachers that ever I attended, never did I meet with one that had such a perfect command of the passions of his audience. In every sermon that I heard him preach, he would sometimes make them ready to burst with laughter, and the next moment drown them in tears; indeed it was scarce possible for the most guarded to escape the effect.' The anti-Methodists, anxious to make Whitefield's power of

[16] Joseph Trapp, *The Nature, Folly, Sin, and Danger of Being Righteous Overmuch* (London, 1739), p. 59.
[17] See *The Expounder Expounded*, p. 11, and Lavington, p. 13.
[18] No account of the satire of Whitefield's publications would be complete without the ironic attack on his sermons by Mr Barnabas, the companion of Parson Adams in Fielding's *Joseph Andrews*. Mr Barnabas chides a bookseller for printing the sermons because Whitefield '. . . would insinuate to the people, that a clergyman ought to be always preaching and praying. He pretends to understand the Scripture literally; and would make mankind believe, that the poverty and low estate, which was recommended to the church in its infancy, and was only temporary doctrine adapted to her under persecution, was to be preserved in her flourishing and established state. Sir, the principles of Toland, Woolston, and all the freethinkers, are not calculated to do half the mischief, as those professed by this fellow and his followers' (Fielding, *The History of Joseph Andrews and His Friend Mr Abraham Adams* [London, n.d.], p. 78).

oratory seem mechanical and theatrical, either explained his eloquence by the fact that he had acted in plays as a child or accused him of being still an actor. The author of *The Expounder Expounded*, using Whitefield's confession that as a child he had played at being a clergyman and imitated the ministers reading prayers, suggested that Whitefield played '. . . the Part of the *Mock-Minister*, before Multitudes of People, with all the Action and Utterance peculiar to the Theatre. This Farce I have seen him perform so to the Life, that some few of the very ignorant Sort, imagined it to be a Sermon, and were ready to fall down and adore the Preacher.'

Whitefield's language with its exaggerated modesty and injudicious metaphor is depicted in the satires as blasphemy.[19] For example, Whitefield had written that his mother's hope that he would bring her comfort, along 'with the circumstance of my being born in an inn, has been often of service to me in exciting my endeavours to make good my mother's expectations, and so follow the example of my dear Saviour, who was born in a manger belonging to an inn'.[20] The author of *The Expounder Expounded* ironically remarked upon the felicity of this parallel: '. . . there is such an exact Similitude between an Inn belonging to a Manger, and a Manger belonging to an Inn, that I can scarcely believe it could possibly fall out without the immediate Interposition of Providence.' A satiric preacher modelled upon Whitefield asks: 'Now where would you have found such another as me? Christ himself was born in a Stable. My Mother kept an

---

[19] A conservative might well have objected to the first sermon preached by Whitefield in Moorfields, which included this passage: 'Oh do not turn a deaf ear to me, do not reject the message on account of the meanness of the messenger! I am a child, a youth of uncircumcised lips, but the Lord has chosen me that the glory might be all His own. . . . But now God has sent a child that cannot speak, that the power may be seen to be not of men but of God . . . and I am persuaded if any of you should be set upon your watch by this preaching, you will have no reason to repent that God sent a child to cry "Behold the Bridegroom cometh." . . .' Cited in A. D. Belden, *George Whitefield: The Awakener*, pp. 69–70. At least some of the reaction to Methodism can be attributed to the striking and occasionally injudicious metaphors of the movement.

[20] Cited in Tyerman, *The Life of the Rev. George Whitefield*, I.4.

Inn; and does not my Birth very much represent his ?'[21] Squintum described himself as 'the substitute of G - d's goodness on earth, who am more worshipp'd by my people than J - - - s himself....'[22] Some satirists, like the author of *The Methodists, an Humorous Burlesque Poem*, parodied Whitefield's sermons:

> *New Lights, Dark Lanthorns!* all attend,
> The Lord his Messenger doth send;
> Mark him in ME—here take this Cup,
> To Night ye shall with *J* - - sup.[23]

Some of the satiric attacks on Whitefield's oratory may have arisen from his ability at gaining contributions. When he pleaded for money for his Georgia orphanage or for other charities, his audience responded warmly. The effect of his preaching on Benjamin Franklin is well known. Franklin, objecting to the location of Whitefield's orphanage, promised himself that Whitefield would get nothing from him, but by the time the preacher's sermon was concluded, Franklin emptied his pockets into the collection.[24] It was this command which Whitefield held over his audience that his enemies objected to.

Some satirists, attacking Whitefield's method of soliciting contributions, claimed that he played upon the emotions of his congregations and that he supplanted reason with enthusiasm. Mr Ranter, in *The Spiritual Minor*, says of Squintum: 'Sir, when he wants to levy a sum upon his congregation, he tells them, in a canting strain, there are four poor widows here in the tabernacle that stand in need of your assistance; he that giveth to the poor, lendeth unto the Lord, or some such cant....' Dr Hunchback, in Charles Johnstone's *Chrysal*, deliberately deceived his congregation. He '... was busied in writing a letter

---

[21] *The Mock-Preacher*, p. 10.
[22] *A Satirical Dialogue between the Celebrated Mr F--te, and Dr Squintum* (London, 1760), p. 10.
[23] See also *The Celebrated Lecture on Heads*, pp. 19–20, where the preacher is undoubtedly Whitefield.
[24] A. D. Belden, *George Whitefield: The Awakener*, p. 80.

to himself, as from a family in distress, for whom he intended to solicit a subscription the next day from his congregation....'[25] Other writers attributed to Whitefield a logical and satirically Christian motive: he sought to make the poor even poorer to ease their way to Heaven. The author of *A Plain and Easy Road* has his Methodist apologist justify the taking of money from the poor: '*Blessed are the poor*, saith he, *for theirs is the*, &c.—Now, if that is the case, the poorer they are, so much the more blessed: and pray are not these poor under very great obligations to our orator [Whitefield] for making them compleatly so?'

Probably the single charity most coupled with Whitefield's name was the orphanage at Savannah, Georgia, called Bethesda. The plan for the orphanage, originated by Charles Wesley, grew out of Whitefield's first voyage to America in 1737–8. Throughout his life, even after the orphanage was completed, Whitefield solicited funds for it. The satirists almost universally suggested that the funds were misused. When the preacher in *The Mock-Preacher* tries to raise money for the orphanage, he warns that it takes some time to get money to Georgia: 'O how will the pretty little Orphans in *Georgia* admire your Charity, and pray for you, *when I give them the Money collected here?* I can't tell indeed how long it will be, before they will have it all; that, you'll allow, must be a Work of Time: for it is a great Way to *Georgia*, and who can tell but that some Accident or other may happen, to prevent my good Design?' The Methodist apologist in *A Plain and Easy Road* ironically points to the orator's use of the funds for Georgia as evidence of his honesty.

After the erection in 1741 of a large shed in Moorfields, which Whitefield called the Tabernacle, and then the replacement of it with a new Tabernacle in 1753,[26] some satirists suggested that all of Whitefield's appeals for offerings were made so that he might have a place to preach. One asserted that Whitefield persuaded the travellers upon his plain and easy

---

[25] Op. cit. p. 173.
[26] John Gillies, *Memoirs of Rev. George Whitefield*, rev. edn (Middletown, 1838), p. 142.

road to the land of bliss '. . . to raise a sum to build a house, call'd a tabernacle, to hold forth in;—for, in frosty or rainy weather, he could not say that he relish'd preaching upon commons, &c., vastly well'.[27] A satirical dialogue between Mr F - - te and Dr Squintum has Squintum bewail that two thousand pounds was brought to F - - te: 'O had they brought it to me—I cou'd have built a t - b - n - cle with half the money, and sav'd the other half for myself.'

Perhaps because of Whitefield's easy mingling with dissenters, non-conformists, and other non-Anglican religious groups and his dislike for what he called 'the partition wall of bigotry and sect-religion,'[28] the conservative saw Whitefield as a force destroying the Church of England. Although he was ordained as an Anglican priest, some called him a dissenter and urged him to leave the Church in name as he had already done in practice. Peter Paragraph characterized Whitefield's Tottenham Court Road Chapel as Squintum's Schism Shop. Generally the satirists depicted Whitefield as inspired by Satan or the Roman Catholics to undermine the Church. For example, in *The Methodists, an Humorous Burlesque Poem*, Satan, planning in Rome with the Catholics to destroy the Church, invokes praise of Whitefield:

> On him ye Catholicks rely,
> He'll do your Business bye and bye,
> To him prepare a *new-form'd Shrine*,
> Let *W - - d* 'mong your *Legends* shine.

The affliction of Methodism and Whitefield was only the most recent that a Job-like Britain must endure.

Finally the satirists accused Whitefield, as they had done Wesley, of numerous indiscretions, vices, and crimes. He was a glutton who only pretended to abstinence, a hypocrite, a seducer of virgins, and even a madman. But these allegations

[27] *A Plain and Easy Road*, pp. 141–2.
[28] Cited in Tyerman, *Life of Whitefield*, I.38.

bear no significant relation to the Whitefield created in the satires.

The satire of Whitefield contrasts sharply with that of Wesley. The Wesleyan satire, although it is often scurrilous and almost always severe, generally attacks Wesley's actions or his beliefs. The satire of Whitefield is half contemptuous and often salacious. It concentrates not upon his beliefs but upon his appearance and mannerisms. Perhaps the course of the satire was moulded by the flamboyance and lack of circumspection of God's dramatist himself,[29] who, except for his insistence on Calvinism, minimized the importance of both doctrines and Church. The George Whitefield of the satires is a grotesque figure, a buffoon—contemptible and ridiculous. A habit of self-exhibition has placed him in the public eye where he indulges in every theatrical trick, even confession of his immoralities, in order to keep attention. Clumsily evil, he is the Ape of Grace and the Archbishop of Humility.[30] His principal characteristic is hypocrisy; thus he bawls sanctimoniously in order to fill his purse. The Whitefield of the satires is almost a comic figure, lewdly squinting at his congregation as he picks their pockets,[31] an obvious charlatan but dangerous to the unsuspecting and the ignorant.

[29] The singularly apt title is given him by King.
[30] Both of these terms are applied to him in *The Methodists, an Humorous Burlesque Poem*, pp. 24, 27.
[31] A reference to a Punchinello show in which Dr Squintum harangues a group of puppets and picks their pockets as they gaze heavenward is given in *A Journal of the Travels of Nathaniel Snip*, pp. 31-2.

CHAPTER NINE

Satire of Other Methodists

IN ADDITION to the concentrated barrages upon the two great leaders of Methodism, John Wesley and George Whitefield, the satirists of Methodism fired occasional salvoes at other Methodists. The satire of these individuals varied considerably with local circumstances. For example, while some of the more controversial Methodists, like William Romaine and Martin Madan in London, were well known and mentioned in general satires of Methodism, others, like Moore Booker, who himself was technically not a Methodist, were attacked in single pamphlets in Dublin and elsewhere.[1]

Interestingly enough the attacks on Methodists other than the two leaders were aimed primarily at the Calvinistic wing— at Romaine, Madan, Rowland and Sir Richard Hill, Augustus Toplady, and others. The Wesleyans, although they were by no means ignored, were less often ridiculed. Even Charles Wesley was seldom satirized, perhaps because he was more conservative than John Wesley and because after his marriage in 1749 he practically gave up itineration. The greater number of attacks on the Calvinists may have been due, first, in part to their more difficult theological position. Although, as the flood of controversial pamphlets witnessed, the Church permitted considerable theological freedom of belief, it was drawn generally to Arminianism rather than to Calvinism. Certainly too the latitudinarian cleric and layman would have found Calvinism far too rigorous and the concept of the possible redemption of all too comforting.

[1] Although I have tried in this chapter to mention the names of all Methodists important enough to be singled out in the principal satires of Methodism, I have not tried to include every Methodist who might be attacked in a single, local publication.

Secondly, the attacks may have centred on the Calvinists because of their conspicuously untactful manner in an age of controversy which, judged by the most tolerant critic, was untactful. Toplady and the Hills were fierce controversialists, and their very ferocity may have won them both renown and notoriety.

The satire of the lesser saints of Methodism, though perhaps it was less personal than that of John Wesley and Whitefield, was scarcely less abusive.

Of the Oxford Methodists, a group that began with four young men and reached a peak of twenty-seven,[2] except for John Wesley and Whitefield only three were singled out by name or by a clearly identifiable reference in the satires. The principal charge made in the satires against Charles Wesley, the most important of these three to Methodism, was that he was a bad poet. The author of *The Love-Feast*, satirically praising John's poetic ability, had artfully damned both brothers as poets:

> For *pious Hymns* thy Genius equals *Quarles*,
> *Seraphic* Partner of thy Brother *Ch - - les*.

John Kirkby, in *The Imposter Detected*, was probably referring to both Wesleys when he wrote: '. . . these two Murderers of Sense as well as Souls are just about as fitly cut out for Poets, as a lame Horse wou'd be for a Rope-dancer.' Benjamin Ingham, one of the Oxford Methodists who went with Wesley on his missionary journey to Georgia but who later became an advocate of Moravian 'stillness', a belief that it is presumptuous for the individual to make any effort to reach God, and who finally left the Methodists, the Church, and the Moravians to set up a church of his own, is satirized as one of the individuals dissenting from the orator in *A Plain and Easy Road:* 'They [the individuals breaking away] would have you believe that theirs is the way, impossible to be missed—clear of thorns and briars

---

[2] Townsend, *et al.*, *A New History of Methodism*, I.147.

—and, by the dint of assurance alone, (there being not a word of truth in it) they have gain'd a great share of passengers, and have got sums of money, which should have fallen to the lot of our *poor* and dear Mr ——. He has some thoughts of proceeding in chancery against *I - - - m*, especially for setting up a turnpike in his road.'³ Westley Hall, the third of the minor Oxford Methodists satirized, who married Wesley's sister Martha and finally deserted her, was, in David Brook's term, 'the Judas of the club'.⁴ Guilty of indiscretions with women of his church,⁵ he was attacked by one satirist whose real target was John Wesley. The ghost of Voltaire meets in the underworld a spectre, who says:

—I'm W - sl - y Hall—
None of your prim, stiff-starch'd Divines—
You know I wrote for *Concubines*;
And what in *Thesis* I maintain'd,
In *Practice* Brother *John* explain'd.⁶

Of the Wesleyan Methodists, none was more severely satirized than Grace Murray, whose near marriage to Wesley made her a particularly apt subject for the satirist. Her first husband, Alexander Murray, a sailor, objected strenuously to her becoming a Methodist but was himself finally converted before his death at sea in 1741, and Mrs Murray became a class leader in the same year. In 1749 Wesley proposed marriage to her as she nursed him during an illness, but the marriage was frustrated by the efforts of Charles Wesley, who disapproved of his brother's choice. Mrs Murray almost immediately married John Bennett, one of Wesley's own preachers. The satire of Mrs Murray emphasized this relationship to Wesley. In *Voltaire's Ghost* Mrs Murray is described as 'Dutch-built, robust, and

---

³ Tyerman, *Life of Wesley*, I.68; Wesley, *Journal*, III.258–61; Townsend, et al., I.156.
⁴ Townsend, et al., *A New History of Methodism*, I.148.
⁵ Wesley, *Journal*, III.327 note.
⁶ *Voltaire's Ghost to the Apostle of the Sinless Foundery*, p. 18.

square', as 'a Sailor's Trull in the days of her *Paganism*'. The satirist then has Mrs Murray explain her meeting with Wesley and pay tribute to him:

> Ordain'd for *Founderies,* or *Cloysters,*
> I charm'd him first with crying Oysters.
> With him *Conversion's* Race I ran—
> Still, still I love the *pious Man.*
> He taught me each FANATIC Art,
> The downcast Look, the frantic Start,
> The one denoting Thought profound,
> The other *Zeal* that spurns the Ground.
> From him I caught the whining Tone,
> The Knack of length'ning out a Groan,
> And making pantomime Grimace
> Pass for a Sign of *inward Grace;*
> With skill distorting ev'ry Feature
> Strongly to mark the New-Born Creature.

The anti-Methodists also attacked some members of the Anglican clergy who were openly allied to Wesleyan Methodism or sympathetic to it. John Fletcher, vicar of Madeley, Shropshire, who was once chosen by Wesley as his successor; Vincent Perronet, vicar of Shoreham, Kent, and a long-time friend of Wesley; and Henry Venn, vicar of Huddersfield, were noticed unfavourably in anti-Methodist attacks. But Moore Booker, vicar of Delvin, Ireland, who, although not a Methodist, permitted Wesley to preach in his church and wrote favourably of the Methodists, received the full force of the attack of *A Letter to the Rev. Mr M - - re B - - k - r, Concerning the Methodists.*[7] Booker, perhaps careless of his language and his figures, praised the Methodists for their success: 'I must declare that my church, at least its Communion table, owes almost nine in ten of its company to their labours, and I can affirm the same of one or

---

[7] Dublin, 1752. Booker is identified as the Reverend Mr Henry Booker by Leslie F. Church, *The Early Methodist People,* p. 5.

two neighbouring parishes.'⁸ His opponent examined his mathematics carefully: 'You acknowledge you owe nine in ten of your communicants to the labours of the methodists, and ... you boast of having no less than seventy. Will it not be asked what sort of clergyman you have been, who could bring but seven persons to the holy sacraments, without the assistance of itinerant preachers?' Then the pamphleteer seized upon Booker's use of the word *company*: 'You call an assembly of christians at the communion table a *company*. Very jovial indeed! But it is usual with most men to give the appellations of things they are most conversant with to those they are less accustomed to. Thus the sailor talks of steering his horse; and Mr B - - - r, I suppose, invites his parishioners to favour him with their company at the communion.'

The attacks on the Calvinistic Methodists, like those on the Wesleyans, struck both priest and layman. Selina, Countess of Huntingdon, probably the highest ranking Methodist, devoted her time and money to the Methodist, but particularly the Calvinistic Methodist, cause. Having been both one of the first Methodists and a strong supporter of the Church, she erected chapels to which she appointed ministers, and in 1768 she established a school, Trevecca College, at which ministers were to be trained. Both popular and influential, she even visited David Garrick at Drury Lane and unsuccessfully urged him to withdraw Foote's *The Minor*.⁹ In the satires Lady Huntingdon, the '*Lady of Trevecka*', is the financial support of the Methodists.¹⁰ By virtue of her position, she provides influence when it is needed. Thus, in a satirical dialogue between F - - te and Squintum, Squintum indicates that he would not object to having Foote murdered: 'Murder! no, no, 'tis only taking him off, and serving him in his own coin.—Besides, never fear the law, we can get over that. There's the C - - of H - - -, and the

---

⁸ Cited in Church, *The Early Methodist People*, p. 5.
⁹ Townsend, *et al.*, *A New History of Methodism*, I.269–70; Mary Belden, *The Dramatic Works of Samuel Foote*, p. 173.
¹⁰ The phrase appears in *The Love-Feast*, p. 16.

L - d D - - -, and my L - - d C - - -, with several other great folks, and the whole society for the R - - - of M - -: I warrant you, the law shan't touch you.'[11] More characteristic of personal satire, Evan Lloyd, the author of *The Methodist*, alleged that the Countess used her preachers to re-awaken her satiated appetites:

> H - - -, cloy'd with *carnal* Bliss,
> Longing to taste how *Spirits* kiss,
> Bids *Chapels* for her *Saints* arise,
> Which are but *Bagnios* in Disguise. . . .

Two Calvinistic Methodist laymen, Sir Richard and Rowland Hill, themselves indulged in considerable promiscuous and controversial publication. Sir Richard, who was not a preacher but who published extensively in the Calvinist controversy, was characterized by a Mr Woolley, chaplain of the Marshalsea, as 'this mighty Richard Hill, this red-hot baronet from the Welch [*sic*] mountains, this independent borough-member. . . .'[12] The baronet, beginning his service to Christianity, '. . . sallied forth from the brothels of Oxford, and the haunts of dissipation, to reform and enlighten mankind! . . .' Rowland Hill, his youngest brother, though a preacher, was never ordained, and after considerable preaching at Lady Huntingdon's London chapels, was set up by his friends in a chapel of his own, Surrey Chapel, Southwark.[13] As a fiery evangelist in the Whitefield tradition Rowland Hill was accused satirically of contributing to insanity and of increasing the number of suicides. Woolley affirmed that the proprietors of private madhouses within twenty miles of London hailed him as their benefactor:

---

[11] *Satirical Dialogue between the Celebrated Mr F--te, and Dr Squintum*, p. 25. The identity of the two lords is not clear. L--d D--- is perhaps the Earl of Dartmouth, who presented Whitefield's plan for a theological college in Georgia to the Archbishop of Canterbury (See A. D. Belden, *George Whitefield: The Awakener*, p. 94). The society, of course, is the Society for the Reformation of Manners.

[12] *A Cure for Canting* . . ., p. 57.

[13] Elliott-Binns, *The Early Evangelicals* . . ., p. 232. Sir Richard attended Magdalen, Oxford; Rowland attended St John's, Cambridge.

From *The Love-Feast, A Poem*, published in London in 1778 and dedicated 'To the Whole Communion of Fanatics That *infest* Great-Britain, and *Artfully* endeavour to shelter themselves under the Wing of *rational Dissention*'.

SATIRE OF OTHER METHODISTS

ROWLAND HILL is in one respect at least unparalleled: he is the only preacher that ancient or modern times have ever yet produced, who could raise his hearers above all those weak fears and childish horrors which nature, reason, and religious prejudices have annexed to acts of suicide. His proselytes have given several proofs that they could smile at the razor's edge or at the halter's noose that was to launch their souls into eternity; and the glowings of love have been so burning hot in some of them, on their return from his evening lectures, that they could find no relief but in the cool bottom of the Thames! Black Friars' Bridge is now become as famous as the *Lover's leap* of old; and many a modern *Sappho*, after chanting one of Rowland's celestial hymns, have plunged with intrepidity into the over-whelming tide.

The Methodist, driven lunatic by Rowland Hill, like Gray's bard flings himself triumphantly to death. Other satires as well testify to Rowland Hill's oratorical fame.

Of the Anglican clergy closely allied to Calvinistic Methodism William Romaine, lecturer at St Dunstan's-in-the-West from 1748 until his death in 1795,[14] and Martin Madan, chaplain of the Lock Hospital, were most often satirized. Romaine, in *The Fanatic Saints*, is characterized as 'a downright *fanatic Quixote*, though once rational, as 'a *Gospel-Labourer* run *mad*'. His enthusiastic preaching of salvation by faith produces strange results:

> *Blest Converts raving*, and *lewd Saints* in *Gangs*,
> Who *penitently* bend to *Prostitution*,
> And *fall*, to *rise new-born* from *Absolution*. . . .

Mad Romano's preaching, as described in *The Love-Feast*, produces very different effects:

> Warm'd with his Subject, he *breaks loose* to serve
> His Cause, with all his Lungs, and ev'ry Nerve;
> Calls up each *corp'ral Agent* to his Aid,
> And of their *Saviour* makes his Flock *afraid*. . . .

[14] *The Early Evangelicals* . . ., p. 164. Elliott-Binns classifies Romaine as an Evangelical rather than a Methodist.

Evan Lloyd, in *The Methodist*, struck by the paradox of salvation by faith alone, attributed to Romaine almost miraculous powers, powers that could invalidate not only natural but supernatural laws as well:

> R - m - - ne works greater *Wonders* still,
> Pulls you by *Gravity* up-*Hill*,
> And for whate'er you do *amiss*,
> Rewards you with *celestial Bliss;*
> By your *bad Deeds* your *Faith* you shew,
> 'Tis but *believe*, and *up You* go.

Martin Madan, once a member of the Hell Fire Club and finally the author of a work advocating polygamy,[15] *Thelyphthora, or a Treatise on Female Ruin,* was often coupled with Romaine in satires of Methodism, probably because both were Calvinists and both were florid preachers. Romaine, in *The Fanatic Saints,* heads 'A *Flock* as *choice* as M - d - n's'. In *The Temple of Imposture* Mahomet tells the Goddess Furina that in tabernacles 'M - - - n, R - - - ne, and W - - - y' mimic him. But often Madan was distinguished. The author of *The Methodist* punned upon Madan's title as chaplain of Lock Hospital as he enumerated the remedies Methodism offered for sick souls:

> *Tottenham's* the best accustom'd *Place,*
> There *Magus* [Whitefield] *squints* Men into *Grace,*
> W - s - - y sells Powders, Draughts, and Pills,
> Sov'reign against all sorts of Ills,
> *Assurance* charms away the Fit,
> Or at least makes it intermit—
> M - d - n the springs of Health *unlocks,*
> And by his Preaching cures the P - -.

The lightest satire of Madan resulted from his publication in 1780 of *Thelyphthora, or a Treatise on Female Ruin,* a defence on scriptural grounds of polygamy. Six days after its publication

---

[15] Lee, *The Lord's Horseman*, p. 81; F. C. Gill, *The Romantic Movement and Methodism*, p. 129.

William Cowper, Madan's cousin, sent to his friend John Newton a mock-heroic poem entitled *Anti-thelyphthora*.[16] In this work a knight, Sir Airy del Castro [Madan], is in love with Dame Hypothesis, who has placed various spells upon her knights. Upon Sir Airy she imposes the strangest: a belief that the marriage bond is not sacred. He maintains:

> That wedlock is not rigorous, as supposed,
> But man, within a wider pale enclosed,
> May rove at will, where appetite shall lead,
> Free as the lordly bull that ranges o'er the mead. . . .[17]

When a quarrel erupted between Newton and Madan, Cowper sent to Newton in the next year the poem 'On Martin Madan's Answer to John Newton's Comments on Thelyphthora'. After ridiculing their quarrel, Cowper wrote:

> Now N. had a wife, and he wanted but one,
> Which stuck in M.'s stomach as cross as a bone;
> It has always been reckoned a just cause of strife,
> For a man to make free with another man's wife,
> But the strife is the strangest that ever was known,
> If a man must be scolded for loving his own.[18]

Other figures—some within the periphery of Methodism and some just beyond—are named in the anti-Methodist attacks. Thomas Jones, chaplain at St Saviour's, Southwark, adopted Methodist doctrines and bombast and won money and fame.[19] The author of *Voltaire's Ghost* cited Augustus Toplady, Wesley's long-time Calvinist adversary, and James Wheatley as authorities for his characterization of Wesley.[20] Griffith Jones,

---

[16] Lodwick Hartley, 'Cowper and the Polygamous Parson', *MLQ*. XVI (1955), p. 138.
[17] *The Poetical Works of William Cowper*, 3 vols. (London, 1896), II.314.
[18] Ibid. II.319.
[19] *Methodism and Popery Dissected and Compared*, pp. 51–2.
[20] Wheatley was a Methodist itinerant preacher until he was expelled for 'indecent behaviour', apparently fornication, by the Wesleys. See Tyerman, *Life of Wesley*, II.121ff. The author of *Voltaire's Ghost* also mentions Maxwell, whom I have been unable to identify. The reference may be to Thomas Maxfield, who was converted by Wesley, but who later separated from the Wesleys. See Wesley, *Journal*, V.7.

rector of Llanddowror, Carmarthenshire, who had been an evangelist since 1709, long before the rise of Methodism, mounted 'the yew tree in the churchyard' and provided Whitefield with a precedent for field preaching.[21] Howell Harris, an unordained preacher and later Whitefield's associate in Wales, was visited by Geoffrey Wildgoose. William Law, the author of *Christian Perfection* and *A Serious Call to a Devout and Holy Life*, who, though not a Methodist, exercised a profound influence upon the young John Wesley, is depicted in *Methodism Triumphant* as a kind of John the Baptist preparing the way for his saint. Finally Count Zinzendorf, leader of the Moravians and founder of the settlement at Herrnhut, which was visited by Wesley, is 'a pickle gentleman, from a mad and obstinate queen's dominions, who said that he was a count', who deviated from the orator's plain and easy road.[22]

In general, the satire of the minor Methodists seems curiously lacking in originality and force. For the clergy the same satiric labels placed on Wesley and Whitefield and even on Methodist preachers in general seem to suffice. These Methodist clergy are simply bombastic and hypocritical. There is no impaling on a pin with an effective phrase, like the reference to John James Heidegger in *The Dunciad*:

> ... (a monster of a fowl,
> Something betwixt a Heideggre and Owl).[23]

Only to Grace Murray, who emerges as a low-class, hypocritical slut, and to Martin Madan, the misguided zealot, is a distinctive satiric reality given. Despite the mention of their names in the satires, the other minor Methodists are shadows, without substance and reality.

[21] *Letter to the Rev. Mr George Whitefield*, p.7.
[22] *A Plain and Easy Road*, pp. 146-7. This is by no means the only reference to the eccentric count in eighteenth-century satire, since the Moravians were ridiculed severely, but the references to him in satire of Methodism occur only infrequently.
[23] *The Dunciad*, Book I.ii.289-90. The effectiveness of these lines is emphasized by Aubrey L. Williams, *Pope's Dunciad: A Study of Its Meaning* (Baton Rouge, 1955), pp. 66-7.

CHAPTER TEN

The Methodists and the Church

THE EIGHTEENTH-CENTURY Methodist's relationship to the Church of England was a complex and confusing one. The average member of a Methodist society considered himself a member of the Church of England, although probably a cut above the other members; yet his principal instruction, since his leaders were forbidden to preach in many of the churches, came not in the parish church on Sunday morning or afternoon but in the fields in the early morning or in a neighbour's house at night, and later in meeting-houses not open during regular church hours. Armed like his fellow-members with a conversion which seemed clearly to mark him as chosen by God, he was perhaps inclined to feel that one who had not experienced such a conversion could not really be called a Christian. Thus often a kind of spiritual arrogance developed, both among leaders and followers. Although the Methodist leaders urged loyalty to the Church, the fact that they themselves assumed that the Church was not performing its proper functions and the fact that the individual Methodist, because of his conversion, was extremely conscious of his spiritual superiority made close ties between the Methodists and the Church unlikely. These things drove a wedge between the Methodists and the Church, since in many cases the parish priest to whose church the Methodists went might well admit that he could not tell when and where he had been born again, even if he did not actually question the authenticity of their experience.

Then the gradual introduction by the Methodists of an unordained ministry, and sometimes an untaught one depending almost solely upon what they believed the guidance and inspiration of the Holy Spirit, led the Methodists to deprecate learning and a learned clergy, for scholarship was of no value without faith. Also the Methodists saw that the men assigned by the Church to be their spiritual guides sometimes led immoral lives and scarcely practised, at least toward the Methodists, what they were expected to preach.

Yet deeply pious, the Methodists sought ways in which to draw themselves closer to God. If the world was too enticing, they would renounce it. Thus a new puritanism—a disdain of such worldly and, the Methodist was sure, such basically evil activities as swearing, dancing, and theatre-going—came into being.

All these things are elements in the highly complex relationship of the Methodist to the Church. The attacks on the clergy and even the puritanism of the Methodists were part of the attempt to purify God's world. Yet inevitably, the satirist, whether he leaped to the defence of the Established Church or simply mocked the righteous overmuch, would ridicule the spiritual arrogance of the Methodists which condemned many of the clergy, presumptuously attacked non-Methodists, and stripped life even of its innocent pleasures.

From the origin of Methodism in 1729 to almost the end of the century the Methodists declared that they were members of the Church of England and that they had no desire to separate from it. The Holy Club itself was simply a religious society in the tradition of Anglican religious societies. As late as 1775 Wesley recorded in his *Journal* that he had visited Congleton, '... where all is now peace and love. None is now left to speak against the Methodists, except Mr Sambach, the curate. He earnestly labours to drive them from the Church, but they will not leave it yet. They both love her Liturgy and her doctrine, and know not where to find better.'[1] From the beginning Methodist services were held at hours when the churches were not open, and in the beginning at least the Holy Communion

---

[1] Wesley, *Journal*, V.450-1.

was celebrated in meeting houses only when the local priest refused to administer the sacrament to the Methodists. Yet even outside the church, the sacrament was celebrated only by a priest of the Church of England.

Yet by 1795 the separation was practically complete. The refusal of the leaders to permit lay preachers to celebrate the sacrament and the closing of the chapels during church hours may have contributed to separation, since the actions drove some Methodists to dissenting bodies, whose services were held at regular church hours.[2] Although one of the rules of the bands '—the innermost circles of the Societies—was that their members should be at Church and Sacrament every week',[3] there is some evidence that the Methodists were gradually dissatisfied with this arrangement. James Lackington, admittedly a somewhat biased contemporary observer, said that Methodists would not go to church but only to Methodist meetings. But certainly the gradual growth of Methodism outside the Church, the formation of societies, and the construction of chapels made separation likely.[4] According to Henry Carter, that separation was made inevitable by three steps: the Deed of Declaration of 1784, which made Methodism a continuing body; Wesley's ordinations of laymen[5]; and licensing of Methodist chapels as dissenting meeting-houses under the Toleration Act.[6] These steps must have made it difficult for the non-Methodist to accept the Methodist insistence that he was an Anglican.

Yet had the Methodists immediately separated, they would probably have been less abused. The anti-Methodists, far from urging the Methodists not to separate, angrily attacked their

[2] T. Jackson, *The Life of the Rev. Charles Wesley*, p. 524.
[3] H. Carter, *The Methodist Heritage*, p. 107.
[4] Carter notes that by 1784 over 300 Methodist chapels had been built (*The Methodist Heritage*, p. 135).
[5] Wesley ordained a total of twenty-seven preachers. His first ordinations were of Richard Whatcoat and Thomas Vasey as elders and Thomas Coke as superintendent on 2nd September 1784 (See Carter, p. 149). Elliott-Binns notes that six students from Trevecca College were ordained by the Rev. William Taylor and other clergy in 1779 (p. 218).
[6] Carter, *The Methodist Heritage*, p. 155.

insistence that they were Church of England members. The author of *A Fine Picture of Enthusiasm*, recognizing that the Methodists were actually dissenters, accused them of trying to be over-zealous Anglicans. One anonymous author, probably Edmund Gibson, Bishop of London, cited the Methodist establishing of societies, the fixing of visitations, and the like, and questioned whether the Methodists had not already set up a new church.⁷ The author of *The Methodists, an Humorous Burlesque Poem* saw the Methodist insistence on remaining within the Church as an insidious Romish and Satanic plot to destroy the Church. Other sects had openly fought the Church, but the Methodists destroyed from within:

> *They with the* Church establish'd *join,*
> *Its Pow'r the more to undermine.*
> By *Rule* they *eat,* by *Rule* they *drink,*
> Do all things else by Rule but *think.*
> Accuse their *Priests* of loose Behaviour,
> To get more in the *Laymens* Favour,
> *Method* alone must guide 'em all,
> Whence METHODISTS, themselves, they call,
> Here I [Satan] my Triumphs fix to come,
> And here shall thou fix thine, O *Rome!*

Probably the most scathing attack on the Methodist, and particularly the Wesleyan, insistence upon the connection of the Methodists with the Church, came from the pen of Rowland Hill, who in his title had satirically called a new Methodist chapel a 'Dissenting Meeting-House'. Hill, primarily attacking Wesley, depicted him as the churchman incarnate: '. . . all are against the *Church*, who testify against the errors and ungodliness of Pope JOHN. They are all dissenters, who dissent from his dissentions. You cannot love the *Church*, unless you go to WESLEY's Meeting-house; nor be a friend to the established Bishops, Priests, and Deacons, unless you admire WESLEY's

---

⁷ *Observations upon the Conduct and Behaviour*, p. 20.

ragged legion of preaching barbers, coblers, tinkers, scavengers, draymen, and chimney-sweepers.'[8]

The clearest indication to the non-Methodist that this Methodist insistence on being Anglican was sheer pretension was the Methodist attack upon the clergy of the established Church. At the same time the Methodist piously proclaimed himself an Anglican, he attacked the clergy as being lukewarm and often corrupt.[9] Whitefield was particularly guilty of this practice.[10] Although Wesley himself was moderate in his criticism, many of his followers were not. But even Wesley's criticism was occasionally vitriolic. He wrote bitingly of the parish priest of South Shields, which Wesley visited in May 1761: 'Why, is there not here (as in every other parish in England) a particular minister who takes care of all their souls? There is one here who takes *charge* of all their souls; what *care* of them he takes is another question. It may be he neither knows nor cares whether they are going to heaven or hell. Does he ask man, woman, or child any question about it from one Christmas to the next? Oh, what account will such a pastor give to the Great Shepherd in that day?'[11] But Wesley wrote later that railing at the clergy never did good and often did harm.[12]

[8] Rowland Hill, *Imposture Detected, and the Dead Vindicated* (London, 1777), p. 21.
[9] It hardly seems necessary to attempt to correct the old view of the eighteenth-century Anglican clergy as being incredibly corrupt. Some undoubtedly were, but many led lives devoted to the Church. Even some of the bishops, who were particularly stigmatized as incompetent, attempted to guide their flocks. Elliott-Binns notes that in 1724 Edmund Gibson, Bishop of London, and later an ardent foe of Methodism, apparently endeavouring to keep Christianity from becoming simply a moral code, urged his clergy to pay more attention '... to the doctrines peculiar to Christianity as "a new way of obtaining forgiveness of sins and a reconciliation with God"...' (p. 116). Even Joseph Trapp, warning his congregation against being righteous overmuch, had another warning to offer them: 'But let us not, to avoid *Enthusiasm*, fall into *Coldness*, or *Lukewarmness* in Religion; nor be *too little righteous*, for Fear of being righteous overmuch' (p. 69). For a sound examination of many of the theological problems of the century, see Roland N. Stromberg, *Religious Liberalism in Eighteenth-Century England* (London, 1954).
[10] Stuart C. Henry, *George Whitefield: Wayfaring Witness* (New York, 1957), p. 133. This charge is frequently made against Whitefield in the non-satiric controversial writing of the eighteenth century.
[11] Wesley, *Journal*, IV.460.   [12] Ibid. V.315-16.

The answer of the non-Methodist defender of the Anglican clergy to charges of immorality and corruption was varied. Officially the Church could point to the twenty-sixth article, which expressly asserted that the validity of the sacraments was not endangered by the evil lives of those administering them. Alexander Jephson, rector of the parish church in Craike, Durham, specifically considered the problem of a dissolute clergy and urged restraint and prayer on the part of Christians: 'In such a Case I beg of you to consider, that the Effects of *Christ's* Ordinances are not in the least impaired, nor the Grace of the Sacraments diminished on Account of their being administered by the Hands of unworthy Men, as our Church hath wisely determined [in] her XXVIth Article.'[13]

Although Jephson's answer and others as well were careful and restrained, the satirists, the effectiveness of whose work depended not upon a reasoned answer to charges but upon an exaggerated restatement of those same charges, ridiculed extensively the Methodist attacks on the clergy and generally attributed to the Methodists attacks on reason and learning as well. Nathaniel Snip, an itinerant Methodist preacher, in his *Journal* brands a clergyman who has rescued him from a mob as 'a pretended Teacher of the Word'. The Methodist ghost, seeking passage across the river to the underworld, refuses to give up a newspaper because it has published his charge against a clergyman. In it, the Methodist says: '. . . I have openly charg'd him with a shameful *Lukewarmness*, and a Spirit of *Preferment-Hunting*. The Scandal of our *modern Clergy*.'[14]

The satiric depiction of Methodist attacks on the reasoning and learning of the Anglican clergy stressed the Methodist's reliance solely upon the Holy Spirit for inspiration. The Calvinistic Methodist preacher in Crabbe's *The Borough* saw a symbolic significance in the clergy's reading of black letter books and ridiculed their uninspired attempt at exegesis:

[13] Alexander Jephson, *A Friendly and Compassionate Address to All Serious and Well Disposed Methodists* (London, 1760), p. 53.
[14] *The London Magazine* (1739), p. 452.

So much to duties; now to learning look,
And see their priesthood piling book on book;
Yea, books of infidels, we're told, and plays,
Put out by heathens in the wink'd-on days;
The very letters are of crooked kind,
And show the strange perverseness of their mind.
Have I this learning? When the Lord would speak,
Think ye he needs the Latin or the Greek?
And lo! with all their learning, when they rise
To preach, in view the ready sermon lies;
Some low-prized stuff they purchased at the stalls,
And more like Seneca's than mine or Paul's.
Children of bondage, how should they explain
The spirit's freedom, while they wear a chain?
They study words, for meanings grow perplex'd,
And slowly hunt for truth, from text to text,
Through Greek and Hebrew—we the meaning seek
Of that within, who every Tongue can speak.[15]

Lancaster's saint in *Methodism Triumphant* singled out a specific clergyman for attack, William Warburton, the Bishop of Gloucester, although he is identified only by title. The bishop,

> ... this Man of Sin,
> Unhappily o'erwhelmed in the Gulph
> Of Human Erudition, and defil'd
> With all the turpitude of carnal sense

is attacked for using 'Wit profane' on 'THE PRINCE OF SAINTS'.[16]

---

[15] *The Borough*, Letter IV.11.359-76.
[16] *Methodism Triumphant*, pp. 15-16. The reference seems clearly to Warburton, who was consecrated as Bishop of Gloucester in 1760, and who published in 1762 an attack on Wesley, *The Doctrine of Grace: or, The Office and Operations of the Holy Spirit Vindicated from the Insults of Infidelity, and the Abuses of Fanaticism*. The reference to the Bishop of Gloucester in *Methodism Triumphant*, published in 1767, theoretically might refer to any one of three bishops: Martin Benson, bishop from 1735 to 1752; James Johnson, 1752-9; and William Warburton, 1760-79. See *Fasti Ecclesiae Anglicane, or A Calendar of the Principal Ecclesiastical Dignitaries in England and Wales, and of the Chief Officers in the Universities of Oxford and Cambridge from the Earliest Time to the Year MDCCXV*, compiled by John Le

As he is converted, he will become a friend to Methodism. He will be 'A GARRICK in the Theatres of Grace'! and shall 'Bethlem's Fields to G - - r's Throne prefer'.

The Methodist insistence upon the necessity of conversion left the religious group open to the charge of spiritual arrogance. Although no Methodist leader was bold enough to assert that the only road to salvation lay on the turnpike of Methodism, the satirists to some extent saw this assumption rising from the Methodist insistence on the necessity of conversion and the fact that such conversions occurred more often within the pale of Methodism than anywhere else. Nathaniel Lancaster's saint calls upon the priests of the church to save themselves but warns that they must turn to Methodism:

> High as you are, to Us you must descend:
> Th' obstetric Med'cines in Our Hands are lodg'd;
> And we, alone, dispense the Heav'nly Boon—
> The Cure infallible for Souls diseas'd.

The meaning is clear; salvation lies only with the saints. Those who have not experienced the obstetric power, 'moral reprobates', are damned. The author of *Perfection* satirically affirmed that the Methodists were the chosen people, that 'A suff'ring *Saviour* dy'd for *them alone*'. Apprenticed to Anabaptists, James Lackington assumed that his master and mistress, though good in all other ways, were children of the devil, and when his master died, Lackington feared that he had gone to hell because he was not a Methodist. Later, after Lackington left Wesley's society and presumably damned himself, he found that Wesley's 'old women' mourned over the backslider: 'Some as they passed by my door in their way to the Foundery would only make a stop and lift up their hands, turn up the whites of their eyes, shake their heads, groan, and pass on.'

Neve and continued by T. Duffus Hardy, 3 vols. (Oxford, 1854), I. 441. Bishop Benson ordained Whitefield as a priest in 1739, and although at one point he regretted the ordination, on his deathbed he sent Whitefield ten guineas and asked that he pray for him. Bishop Johnson apparently played no important role in the Methodist controversy.

The spiritual arrogance of the Methodists is also illustrated in the satires by the Methodist scorn for the non-Methodist, exemplified by such terms as the Almost Christian, the Moral Reprobate, and the Nominal Christian, and the assigning of non-Methodists, particularly anti-Methodists, but sometimes even Methodists who disagreed with other Methodists, to Hell. One satiric author explained the phrase '*almost Christians*, who fall short of *Grace*', as 'A contemptuous Name among the *Saints* for all but their own *mad* Sect'.[17] Squintum, in *A Satirical Dialogue*, arrogates post-chariots only for Methodists: 'Hath he [Foote], or any one else out of the pale of methodism, the least right to a post-chariot? I have, it is true, such a conveniency to facilitate my holy labours; but in one of the wicked, it is pride, I say, it is vanity; nay more, it is presumption.' Lancaster's saint in *Methodism Triumphant* imagines that those sinners condemned to the hottest flames of Hell are the anti-Methodists:

... They reason'd, and they laugh'd:
And now they weep—now ever must weep on.

The Methodist summoning of those who opposed them to the bar of judgement becomes in the satires part of the Methodist scorn for the anti-Methodist. Nathaniel Snip angrily cited a priest to the bar of judgement who spoke of the value of good works: 'I cannot, 'tis true, punish thee in this World as thou deservest; but take Notice, take Notice, Friend *W - -* I summon thee to answer this at the Barr of the Most High, where I shall be thy Accuser for these Unchristian Blasphemies.' But Lancaster satirized a specific summons issued by Wesley, who had recorded the incident in his *Journal* for 2nd April 1740: 'Calling at Newgate in the afternoon, I was informed that the poor wretches under sentence of death were earnestly desirous to

[17] *Sketches for Tabernacle-Frames*, p. 28. The term probably came from Wesley's famous sermon preached at St Mary's, Oxford, 25th July 1741, on the text, 'Almost thou persuadest me to be a Christian'. Wesley, *Journal*, II.478–81.

speak to me, but that it could not be, Alderman [Michael] Beecher having just then sent an express order that they should not. I cite Alderman Beecher to answer for these souls at the judgement-seat of Christ.' Lancaster ironically compared the sin of Beecher with those of the felons:

> ... But know, O Wretch!
> The Sentence of the Saint will be confirm'd;
> And thou must answer for this Loss of Souls.
> Burn! BEECHER! burn! in fiercer flames involv'd,
> As thy Offence so far surpasses theirs.

The satirists also criticized Methodist attacks on books, like Whitefield's attack on *The Whole Duty of Man*, first printed in 1675,[18] and particularly satirized the Calvinistic and Wesleyan Methodist disagreements.

The new puritanism of the Methodists, rising out of their zeal to live holy and unsullied lives, led them to attack what Lackington called 'rational pleasures'. This new puritanism led them to strict keeping of the Sabbath, opposition to dancing, reprimanding others for swearing, and attacks on theatre-going. Such strictness concerning what the non-Methodist generally considered harmless diversions invited ridicule.

Some of the attacks ridiculed Methodist strictness generally. Bishop Lavington, for example, described the ingredients that made up a true Methodist: 'He must set out on *Foot*, with a *sanctified Countenance*, and high *Pretences to Piety*; which is to consist of *unscriptural Peculiarities, whimsical Strictnesses*, and *bitter Zeal against innocent and indifferent Things.*'[19] Foreseeing the new world when Methodism would triumph, Nathaniel Lancaster depicted a world untainted by such pleasures as balls, concerts, dancing, and cards. One provocative bit of satire, although it ridiculed Methodist dress, was probably intended as a general explanation of Methodist puritanism. Lady Lam-

---
[18] Elliott-Binns, *The Early Evangelicals*, p. 402.
[19] *The Enthusiasm of Methodists . . .*, pp. 350–51.

bert, in *The Hypocrite*, insists that her daughter remove the lace at her neck and wear muslin. She explains: 'Doctor Cantwell complains to me that he cannot sit at table, the sight of her bare neck disturbs him so; and he's a good man, and knows what indecency is.'[20]

Although in eighteenth-century Britain Sunday was generally rather loosely observed, with shops remaining open, the Methodists and Evangelicals kept its sanctity rigorously. Rowland Hill, whose congregation was well indoctrinated, was once criticized for driving to church in his carriage on Sunday. William Grimshaw, a friend of the Wesleys, rector at Haworth, forbade the playing of football on Sunday and insisted on regular attendance at church. Wesley in 1745 published a four-page pamphlet on the subject: *An Earnest Persuasive to Keep the Sabbath Holy*. Tyerman reported that the Methodist Conference in 1782 agreed that members of the Methodist societies would not have their hair dressed on Sunday and would not participate in military exercises on Sunday as volunteers or spectators.[21]

The satirists depicted the Methodists as going to ridiculous extremes to maintain the holiness of the Sabbath. Mr Loader tries to cheer up Jenny Cummins, whom he has ruined: 'Why, Child, if you behave in the same Manner to your Customers, you'll soon have no Lovers, but a Set of Hypocritical Methodists, or some of the Society for the Reformation of Manners, who will inform against a poor Woman for endeavouring to maintain herself and Half a Dozen Children by Selling a Basket of Apples on a Sunday Evening.'[22] Lackington claimed that a Methodist was supposed to have '. . . staved a barrel of beer in his cellar, because he detected it *working* on the Sabbath day'. Colonel Lambert, in *The Hypocrite*, speaking of Cant-

---

[20] Isaac Bickerstaff, *The Hypocrite*, p. 36.
[21] Elliott-Binns, *The Early Evangelicals*, pp. 443, 150–51; Tyerman, *Life of Wesley*, III.372.
[22] [Israel Pottinger] *The Methodist, a Comedy* (3rd edn, London [1761]), p. 11.

well's warm disposition, says of the hypocrite: 'In the country he used to make the maids lock up the turkey cocks every Saturday night, for fear they should gallant the hens on a Sunday.'

The Methodist prohibition of dancing (no one was permitted to remain in a Methodist society who danced or played cards)[23] and the reproving of swearers were mildly satirized. One satirist imagined the London Methodist preachers voting to determine whether or not dancing was sinful. The result was not unexpected:

> They voted that dancing's a terrible sin,
> That all manner of vice by that means was let in;
> 'Twas a crime, they declar'd, without benefit of clergy;
> And after this sin they'd no pills that cou'd purge ye....[24]

Wesley recorded, not without wit, in his *Journal* for 23rd March 1743 one occasion when he reproved a swearer: 'I met a gentleman in the streets cursing and swearing in so dreadful a manner that I could not but stop him. He soon grew calmer; told me he must treat me with a glass of wine; and that he would come and hear me, only he was afraid I should say something against fighting of cocks.' As the less fortunate Geoffrey Wildgoose reprimanded some men in Birmingham for swearing, 'one of them emptied the stale contents of an unscowered piss-pot upon the heads of him and his companions'.[25]

The Methodist attitude toward the theatre had never been particularly friendly, although John Wesley had been interested in the theatre in his younger days.[26] But with the appearance of *The Minor* and the group of similar plays, the Methodist attitude hardened. A clerical opponent of Foote, probably Martin

---

[23] Leslie F. Church, *The Early Methodist People*, pp. 215-16.
[24] *Transactions of the London Methodist Parsons. In Three Poetical Epistles* (London, 1792), pp. 2-3.
[25] Graves, *The Spiritual Quixote* . . ., II.122.
[26] For one account of the Methodists and the theatre, largely a report on the plays featuring Whitefield, see T. B. Shepherd, 'Methodists and the Theatre in the Eighteenth Century', *Proceedings of the Wesley Historical Society*, XX (1935-6), pp. 166-85, XXI (1937-8), pp. 3-7.

Madan, referring to Foote's allegation that the opponent knew nothing of the theatre, responded with what was a common Methodist reaction: 'Mr Foote tells me I have shown myself absolutely ignorant of the nature of the theatre, and the drama. I glory in that ignorance! I bless God, my studies have run in a very different track.'[27] Four years later, in 1764, John Wesley protested on both moral and commercial grounds to the mayor and corporation against the plan to build a new theatre in Bristol.[28]

The satirists attribute to their Methodist characters such denunciations of the playhouse as 'that cursed Place' and 'the devil's hot-bed'.[29] Squintum, in a satirical dialogue with F - - te, is assured by the mimic that God will destroy the playhouse as the evangelist has prayed. The dramatic satirists of Methodism, particularly Foote, may expect their punishment hereafter. Lancaster prophesied in *Methodism Triumphant* that Hell, the mimic's destination, will have no playhouses:

> No Farces there, no bursts of jovial Glee;
> Nor Methodists on whom to vent your Gibes.

Even those who attend playhouses, warns Dr Squintum as he speaks the epilogue to *The Spiritual Minor*, will be damned: 'They then will clap 'midst weeping and 'midst wailing. . . .' But one of the most telling satires of the Methodist attitude toward playhouses, a song sung by Squintum in *The Methodist, a Comedy*, explains the reason for that attitude:

I

> Ye pious Servants that resort
> Where Faith a precious Harvest yields,
> Who sweetly grunt at *Tottenham-Court*,
> Or loudly snivel at *Moorfields*.

---

[27] [Martin Madan] *An Exhortatory Address to the Brethren in the Faith of Christ* (London, 1760), p. 11.
[28] Tyerman, *Life of Wesley*, II.514.
[29] *The Methodist, a Comedy*, p. 62; Isaac Bickerstaff, *The Hypocrite*, p. 23.

METHODISM MOCKED

II

In me securely put your Trust,
And I shall still direct your Ways;
But then you must renounce the Lust,
The fond Desire of seeing Plays.

III

For Satan in this wicked Age
Employs the Force of all his Arts,
And makes that cursed Place the Stage
A Bait to snap up Human Hearts.

IV

To see an idle Fellow play,
The giddy town unthinking runs;
Who leads our Daughters all astray,
And hurts the Morals of our Sons.

V

Three Shillings! what a Sum you pay,
A single Play with Ease to see;
When half the Money will defray
Three Months Expense in hearing me.

VI

My Brethren, Warning take by them,
And shun th' impending Wrath betimes;
Your Vanities I must condemn,
Altho' I may excuse your Crimes.

VII

The crooked Paths of Folly shun,
Of Plays and Players hate the Tribe;
To me and to my Doctrine run,
You know the ready way—SUBSCRIBE.

THE METHODISTS AND THE CHURCH

The satiric account of the Methodists' relationship to the Church, to fellow Anglicans, and even to fellow Methodists centres upon essentially one theme—the spiritual arrogance of the Methodist. In the satirist's view, the Methodist, after the emotional upheaval of his conversion, assumes the garment of infallibility. He asserts a maddening experience like his own to be necessary for salvation; he has only contempt for the Anglican priest, whom he considers non-Christian and actually vicious; he refers scornfully to the non-Methodist as the moral reprobate or the Almost Christian; and from his Sinai he brings down a new set of commandments: Thou shalt not swear, thou shalt not dance, but particularly thou shalt not go to playhouses, where Methodists are likely to be reviled.

CHAPTER ELEVEN

The Conventions of the Satires

OF THE VAST body of the literature of anti-Methodism, a considerable part is primarily theological—sermons, admonitions, exhortations, and the like. Although within these works an occasional arrow of ridicule is directed at the Methodists as the cleric-author delivers what he is certain will be a deadly blow at the Achilles heel of the movement, the principal satiric attacks on Methodism come not in these homiletic and polemic works but in relatively formal literary satires modelled on *Hudibras, MacFlecknoe, The Dunciad, A Tale of a Tub,* and other works. These satires, more literary than theological in nature, reveal the techniques or conventions which the anti-Methodists employed and their basic attitudes toward the movement.

Basil Willey has observed that one of the aims of the satirist is 'to trick us into seeing actual and familiar conditions as if for the first time, or as though we were visitors from some Utopian planet, or from China, Persia, or any other supposed headquarters of Reason'.[1] Similarly, Maynard Mack, in discussing the speakers in Pope's formal satires, calls one of them the *ingénu* or the *naïf*. He then explains: 'As *naïf*, the satirist educates us. He makes us see the ulcer where we were accustomed to see the rouge. He is the child in the fairy story for ever crying, "But mamma, the king *is* naked".'[2] Although in the satire of Methodism there are no citizens of the world, not even any returned Gullivers, and certainly no innocents to cry out unabashed the truth that their parents are afraid to see, the

[1] *The Eighteenth-century Background* (London, 1946), p. 104.
[2] Maynard Mack, 'The Muse of Satire', *Yale Review*, XLI (1951), p. 91.

satirists of Methodism used a similar literary device. Armed with a penetrating sophistication, a worldly wisdom, they attempted to remove the blinkers from the eyes of their readers so that their range of vision might be increased—to reveal the religious zeal of the Methodists as hypocritical skullduggery. Thus the author of *Fanatical Conversion*, in dedicating his work to 'The Chief Apostle and Hierophant of that Second Temple of Methodism, The Sinless Foundery', alleged that it was written by 'one of the most Observant of his [Wesley's] Audience'. A few, like the author of *Genuine and Secret Memoirs Relating to the Life and Adventures of That Arch Methodist, Mr G. W - fi - d*, asserted that they could give the reader the truth behind the fraudulent appearance. Other satirists sought to reveal Methodism in its true light by relating it, through their sophistication, to things opposed by Methodism or scarcely flattering to it. Thus, one satirist suggested that a group of fortune-tellers had as much right to practice their art as their fellow-conjurers, Methodists, had; another had a mountebank doctor propose an alliance with a fellow-mountebank, a Methodist preacher. In both satires, the satirists imposed a new point of view upon their readers: the Methodists are no longer seen as pious and righteous men but as charlatans and mountebanks. Other satirists, utilizing the Methodist antipathy toward the theatre, depicted the religious revival as another variety of dramatic entertainment. One satirist had Whitefield, the 'Manager of the Theatre in Tottenham-Court', the Tabernacle, complain indignantly to the 'Manager of the Theatre in the Hay-Market' about the satiric portrayal of Squintum in *The Minor*.[3] Another, *The Mock-Preacher*, only slightly more subtle, depicted a Methodist holding forth on Kennington-Common, a usual place for field preaching. The sub-title of the play reveals that field preaching is simply another kind of dramatic performance: *A Satyrico-Comical-Allegorical Farce. As It Was Acted to a Crowded Audience at Kennington-Common, and Many*

[3] See *A Letter of Expostulation*.

Other Theatres. The same comparison of Methodism with the theatre to give the reader a new perspective is employed by the author of *The Expounder Expounded*, who attributed to Whitefield an inordinate passion for acting: '. . . we have seen him, rather than not act at all, erect himself upon a *Cricket* in *Moorfields*, and play the part of the *Mock-Minister*, before Multitudes of People, with all the Action and Utterance peculiar to the Theatre. This Farce I have seen him perform so to the Life, that some few of the very ignorant Sort, imagined it to be a Sermon, and were ready to fall down and adore the Preacher.' Thus the satirists of Methodism sought to give their readers new perspectives, to enable them to see perhaps for the first time behind the pious mask of Methodism.

There is little evidence that the satirists of Methodism actually sought to give verisimilitude or even any illusion of reality in their depiction of Methodists and Methodism. An occasional writer, like Lackington, asserted that his depiction represented reality: '. . . I have invariably had in view to "speak of them [the Methodists] as they are: nothing to extenuate, nor set down ought in malice".' But most made no attempt to create an illusion of reality or to portray Methodism as it existed in eighteenth-century England. Almost all of them, however, emphasized that the basic incidents used in the satires were true and offered supporting evidence. Some satirists, like the author of *Perfection*, asserted that if the truths they revealed were made public among the Methodists many seemingly unrelated evils would be remedied:

> Were *Truths*, like these at the *lewd F - y* sold
> Its *wooden God* must fail of such Success;
> The Swarms of *Magdalens* wou'd soon grow less;
> The *Bankrupt-List* decrease; and fewer Yells
> Be heard within *Old Bedlam's* frantic Cells. . . .

A few satires, like *The Story of the Methodist-Lady*, purported to be 'True History'; the truth of this story, according to the advertisement, was vouched for by the surgeon who attended the emasculated lover of the Methodist lady. Many, like *Fanatical Conversion*, which asserted that it was 'Illustrated and verified by NOTES from J. WESLEY'S Fanatical JOURNALS', cited the *Journals* of Whitefield and Wesley and other Methodist publications as proof of their charges.[4] The author of *The Temple of Imposture*, justifying his attribution of a Mohammedan 'Spirit of *Tyranny, Lust, Avarice, Persecution,* and *Imposture*' to Wesley, wrote: 'I appeal for the Truth of this Suggestion, to the modern *Calm Addresses*, from *Printing-Presses, Rostrums,* and *Joint-Stools,* in open Fields. . . .' The satirists of Methodism attempted then to convince their audience that the basis of the satires, although they were clothed in the garb of fiction, was true.

Although some satirists indulged simply in more or less witty pejorative fulminations against the Methodists, most developed fairly elaborate narrative fictions centering upon a Methodist hero. The use of this hero or rogue, to be more exact, permitted the satirists then to chronicle a series of adventures parallel in exaggerated form to incidents from Methodist journals or to sketch scenes of debauchery presided over by a Satanic figure urging his followers to greater and greater excess. As these uses imply, the Methodist hero of the satires was generally either an illiterate misled Quixotic wretch or a sinister Machiavellian seducer. In most of the satires the Methodist lay preachers were depicted as Quixotes. Basically good, although lazy, they had fallen easy prey to enthusiasm and fanaticism because of their lack of education and proper guidance. Even their names reflect their gullibility—Ezekiel Daw of Cumberland's *Henry* and Geoffrey Wildgoose of Graves's *The Spiritual Quixote*. The best example of the Methodist hero is Smollett's Humphry Clinker, who, like the others in the category, is a victim of

[4] The passage is taken from the title page. The use of such citation is characteristic of almost all the satires, but see particularly *Journal of the Travels of Nathaniel Snip, Methodism Triumphant,* and Graves's *Spiritual Quixote*.

superstition and fanaticism until he gains knowledge and some social standing. A few of the Methodist lay preachers, generally of the Quixote type, are characterized by their names which reveal the useful trades they have deserted to become teachers of the word—Strap was a shoemaker; Nathaniel Snip was a tailor's apprentice; Shadrach Bodkin was a tailor.[5]

But most of the satiric portraits of individual Methodists, particularly the barely disguised ones of the Methodist leaders, are of evil figures who are motivated by lust or desire for wealth or who are inspired by a diabolic or anti-Christian god. The names once again are largely indicative of the characterization. Dr Cantwell, a name used for both Whitefield and Wesley in various works, is an unctuous hypocritical lecher[6]; Magus is a fiendishly inspired sorcerer, who '*squints* Men into *Grace*'[7]; Reynardo is foxlike, skilful, and cunning in deceit.[8] Others, given names which clearly relate them to the Methodist leaders, are quite as evil. Dr Squintum, who appears frequently in the satires, is a hypocrite who easily reconciles the carnal and the spiritual through the convenient doctrine of justification by faith; his squint becomes almost a Cain-like brand of his evil. Mr Watchlight, with its close verbal parallel to *watch-night*, is avaricious.[9] Such titles as 'the mock preacher', the 'orator', and the 'saint', along with undisguised spellings like Wh - tf - d and W - y, give a slight appearance of fictional portrayal while they give the satirists an obvious opportunity to depict Wesley and Whitefield as charlatans.

Other Methodists who appear in the satires are characterized as lechers, whores, procuresses, and the like. The exaggeratedly feminine names of Corinna and Terentilla, ardent Methodist converts, imply their profession; Mrs Cole, Mrs Snarewell, and Mrs Brimstone are able, at the same time, to be Methodists

[5] See *Fanatic Saints, Ranae Comicae Evangelizantes, Journal of the Travels of Nathaniel Snip*, and Samuel Foote's *The Orators*.
[6] See *The Hypocrite, The Love-Feast*, and *Perfection*.
[7] *The Methodist*, p. 36.
[8] *The Love-Feast, Voltaire's Ghost to the Apostle of the Sinless Foundery*.
[9] *The Register-Office*.

and run houses of prostitution. Lady Harridan, in Coventry's *Pompey the Little*, is little more than her name implies.

In order to make the evil of these thinly disguised Methodists as obvious as possible, the satirists, influenced by the mock-epic tradition, depicted them paying tribute to Satan, to Rome, to Venus, and similar masters or acting as tools, sometimes knowingly, of these. Magus, for example, in *The Methodist*, swears allegiance to Satan; the fiend himself at a conclave in Rome, in *The Methodists, an Humorous Burlesque Poem*, announces that he has created the Methodists in order to destroy the Church of England. The author of *A Wolf in Sheep's Cloathing*, satirically attempting to learn the identity of the author of *A Calm Address*, attributes the pamphlet to a Jesuit ghost. The saint in *Methodism Triumphant*, although he owes his principal allegiance to Phantasia, is described in a parody of Milton's Satan on his throne in hell:

> High on his throne, so when the Awful Saint
> Stands forth, his vocal powers to exercise,
> And drive Transgressors from th'infernal Path;
> So loud he thunders. . . .

Reynardo, in *The Love-Feast*, is ruled over by Murcia. Wesley, in *The Temple of Imposture*, makes obeisance to the goddess Furina, apparently the apotheosis of confusion and discord. Finally a whole group of satires attempted, through a kind of guilt by association, to link Methodism to Mohammedanism. In *Methodism Triumphant* the doctrine of perfection is held in common by the saint and Mohammed. In *The Temple of Imposture* Mohamet intercedes for the Methodists with the goddess Furina:

> In servile imitation of *my* Plan,
> *Priests* now in *Tabernacles* fish for Man.
> There, to thy honour, Goddess, thou canst see
> M - n, R - ne, and W - y, mimic *me*.

METHODISM MOCKED

Despite the variety in style and tone of the anti-Methodist satires, the general attitudes expressed by the satirists toward the movement seem to fall into two categories. These differing attitudes are reflected in the two basically different Methodist heroes. In the same way that one group of satires depicted the Methodists, particularly the lay preachers, as basically good individuals seduced by enthusiasm, and another depicted the Methodists as Satanic figures, one group of the satires seems to view the Methodists tolerantly, to see them as misled Christians who through education and guidance can be made into useful citizens, and the other to see them as rogues, as aberrations, as throwbacks to an era of superstition and bigotry who seek to undermine the authority of reason. For example, Geoffrey Wildgoose, for at least the space of his summer's ramble, is said to have been under 'the influence of a deluded imagination'.[10] Yet as he regains his senses, his spiritual adviser, Dr Greville, urges him to retain his religious zeal: 'Not that I wish to see you less serious in the practice of religion, nor even less an enthusiast, in some sense, as I am convinced nothing great can be effected without some degree of enthusiasm. . . .'[11] Similarly Humphry Clinker, through education, comes to disbelieve the wildest vagaries of Methodism but at the same time maintains a high seriousness in his religious faith. Thus one group of satirists seems to consider Methodists as only slightly over-zealous individuals who need education and a correcting hand. In contrast, other satirists saw Methodism as a retrogression to barbarism and superstition or a dangerous malignancy. Seen from this point of view, the Methodists were not foolish lost sheep to be brought back into the fold but were wolves in sheep's clothing trying to enter the fold by stealth. The author of *Fanatical Conversion*, depicting the war waged by hypocrisy upon '*Virtue, Truth, Simplicity*, and *Sense*', asserted that all of these were harmed by Methodism: '*Virtue*, on ravishing Watch-Nights, and Love Feasts—*Truth*, by wresting the Gospel to

[10] Graves, *The Spiritual Quixote*, II.275.   [11] Ibid. II.260.

selfish Ends—*Simplicity*, by misleading harmless, innocent Novices—*Sense*, by a daring insult on human Understanding.' Hypocrisy, through Methodism, had defiled the fountain of Scriptures 'with foul Stains' and driven a '*tolerating*' nation insane. The author of *The Methodist, a Poem* saw the success of the Methodists and the corruption of reason as evidence of a primeval flaw in human intelligence:

> Why shou'd the Muse of *Angels* tell
> Turn'd into *Devils* when they fell?
> Why search the Chronicles of *Hell*,
> While *Earth* examples it as well?
> Why talk of *Satan*, while we see
> Each day some new Apostacy.

This view of Methodism culminates in the ironic ending of *Methodism Triumphant*. Here, after he has torn off Satan's tail, the saint of Methodism, ironically the Christ who is to come, forces Satan back into Hell. As a choir comes down from Heaven, the gates opened by Sin and Death are triumphantly locked:

> ... Clos'd are the Gates:—
> And thence he [Satan] never can emerge again.

With the presence of Satan in the world obvious, the triumph of Methodism, although ironically stated, is like the restoration of Chaos at the end of *The Dunciad*:

> Lo! thy dread Empire CHAOS! is restored;
> Light dies before thy uncreating word;
> Thy hand, great Anarch! lets the curtain fall,
> And universal Darkness buries All.[12]

[12] Book IV.ii.653–6.

Bibliography

Primary Bibliography

An Additional Scene to the Comedy of the Minor, London, 1761.

[Anstey, Christopher] *The New Bath Guide: or, Memoirs of the B - - n - - r - d Family in a Series of Poetical Epistles*, new edn, London, 1794.

An Apology for the Parishioners of St Dunstan's in the West, for Refusing the Use of Their Pulpit, Any Longer to the Rev. Mr Romaine, Their Late Lecturer, in Which the Fact Is Impartially Stated, and Their Proceedings Vindicated, from the Charge of Oppression, Tyranny, and Irreligion, with Which They Have Been Plentifully Aspersed, London, n.d. [1759].

'An Appendix Giving an Account of the People Called Methodists. By the Translator,' in O. C. Formey, *An Ecclesiastical History from the Birth of Christ to the Present Time*, trans. from French, 2 vols, London, 1766.

[B., A.] *An Earnest and Affectionate Address to the People Called Methodists*, 2nd edn, London, 1745.

Bate, James, *Methodism Displayed; or, Remarks upon Mr Whitefield's Answer, to the Bishop of London's Last Pastoral Letter*, 2nd edn, London, n.d.

[Berridge, John] *Justification by Faith Alone: Being the Substance of a Letter from the Rev. Mr B - - ge in Cambridgeshire, to a Clergyman in Nottinghamshire; Giving an Account of a Great Work of God Wrought in His Heart, Etc. To Which Is Added, by Way of Preface, a Word or Two upon Justification by Faith, and How Affected in an Instantaneous Manner, Etc.*, 2nd edn, London [1758].

Bickerstaff, Isaac, *The Hypocrite, a Comedy Altered from C. Cibber*, London, 1792.

Boswell's Life of Johnson Together with Boswell's Journal of a Tour to the Hebrides and Johnson's Diary of a Journey into North Wales, ed. George B. Hill, rev. edn by L. F. Powell, 6 vols, Oxford, 1934.

Boswell's London Journal, 1762-3, ed. Frederick A. Pottle, New York, 1950.

[Boswell, James] *Observations, Good or Bad, Stupid or Clever, Serious or Jocular, on Squire Foote's Dramatic Entertainment, Intitled The Minor. By a Genius*, Edinburgh, 1760.

Bowden, Samuel, *Poems on Various Subjects; with Some Essays in Prose, Letters to Correspondents, &c., and a Treatise on Health*, Bath, 1754.

BIBLIOGRAPHY

Bull, Patrick, *A Wolf in Sheep's Cloathing: or, An Old Jesuit Unmasked. Containing an Account of the Wonderful Apparition of Father Petre's Ghost, in the Form of the Rev. John Wesley. With Some Conjectures Concerning the Secret Causes That Moved Him to Appear at This Very Critical Juncture*, Dublin printed, London reprinted [1775].
The Poems of Henry Carey. Edited Frederick T. Wood. London [1930].
'Charon and Mercury: or, The Elysian Ferryman. A Dialogue after the Manner of Lucian, in Which Several Others Speak', *The London Magazine: and Monthly Chronologer* [VIII] (1739), 449–53.
Chatterton, Thomas, *The Poetical Works of Thomas Chatterton*, ed. W. W. Skeat, 3 vols, London, 1905.
Church, Thomas, *A Serious and Expostulatory Letter to the Rev. Mr George Whitefield on Occasion of His Late Letter to the Bishop of London, and Other Bishops; and in Vindication of the Observations upon the Conduct and Behaviour of a Certain Sect Usually Distinguished by the Name of Methodists, Not Long Since Published*, London, 1744.
Churchill, Charles, *The Poetical Works of Charles Churchill*, ed. George Gilfillan, Edinburgh, 1855.
A Conversation between Richard Hill, Esq; the Rev. Mr Madan, and the Superior of a Convent of English Benedictine Monks at Paris, Held at the Said Convent, July 13, 1771; in the Presence of Thomas Powis, Esq; and Others, Relative to Some Doctrinal Minutes, Advanced by the Rev. Mr John Wesley and Others, at a Conference Held in London, August 7, 1770. To Which Are Added Some Remarks by the Editor, and the Minutes Themselves Prefixed. As Also Mr Wesley's Own Declaration Concerning His Minutes Versified, by Another Hand, London, 1772.
Coventry, Francis, *The History of Pompey the Little, or, The Life and Adventures of a Lap-Dog*, intro. Arundell del Re, Waltham, Saint Lawrence, 1926.
The Poetical Works of William Cowper, 3 vols, London, 1896.
Crabbe, George, *The Borough*, in *Poems*, ed. A. W. Ward, Cambridge, 1905.
Cumberland, Richard, *Henry*, in *Ballantyne's Novelist's Library*, Vol. IX, London, 1824.
Doctor Trapp Vindicated from the Imputation of Being a Christian, Occasioned by a Pamphlet of the Reverend Author against the Methodists, Intitled The Nature, Folly, Sin, and Danger of Being Righteous Over-much, London, 1739.
[Dodd, William] *A Conference between a Mystic, an Hutchinsonian, a Calvinist, a Methodist, a Member of the Church of England, and*

Others, Wherein the Tenets of Each Are Freely Examined and Discussed, London, 1761.

Downes, John, *Methodism Examined and Disposed: or, The Clergy's Duty of Guarding Their Flocks against False Teachers*, London, 1759.

'A Dozen of Reasons Why the Sect of Conjurers, Called Fortune-Tellers, Should Have at Least as Much Liberty to Exercise Their Admirable Art, as Is Now Granted to Methodists, Moravians, and Various Other Sorts of Conjurers', *The London Magazine: or, Gentlemen's Monthly Intelligencer*, XXVI (1757), 483–4.

An Enquiry after New Lights, Innovators, and Enthusiasts, &c., in a Letter to the Reverend Thomas Jones, A.M., Chaplain of St Saviour, Southwark. Occasioned by His Sermon Preach'd at Bishopsgate and Published at the Request of the Rector, London, 1755.

Entwisle, Joseph, *A Letter to the Author of an Anonymous Treatise on Inspiration*, York, 1799.

An Essay on the Character of Methodism in Which the Leading Principles of that Sect: the Aids It Has Borrowed from the Writings of the Clergy, and the Influence It Has Communicated to Them, Are Considered and Stated, Cambridge, 1781.

Evans, Theophilus, *The History of Modern Enthusiasm, from the Reformation to the Present Times*, 2nd edn, London, 1757.

The Fanatic Saints; or, Bedlamites Inspired. A Satire, London, 1778.

Fanatical Conversion; or, Methodism Displayed. A Satire. Illustrated and Verified by Notes from J. Wesley's Fanatical Journals, and by the Author, Unravelling the Delusive Craft of That Well-Invented System of Pious Sorcery Which Turns Lions into Lambs, Called, in Derision, Methodism, London, 1779.

[Fawcett, Richard] *An Expostulatory Letter to the Rev. Mr Wesley Occasioned by His Address to the Clergy*, London, 1757.

Fielding, Henry, *An Apology for the Life of Mrs Shamela Andrews*, ed. Sheridan W. Baker, Jr, Berkeley and Los Angeles, 1953.

———, *The History of Joseph Andrews and His Friend Mr Abraham Adams*, London, n.d.

———, *The History of Tom Jones, a Foundling*, New York, 1943.

A Fine Picture of Enthusiasm, Chiefly Drawn up by Dr John Scott, Formerly Rector of St Giles's in the Fields. Wherein the Danger of the Passions Leading in Religion is Strongly Described. To Which is Added, an Application of the Subject to the Modern Methodists, Exposing the Principles and Practices of All Such, London, 1744.

Foote, Samuel, *Apology for The Minor, in a Letter to the Rev. Mr Baine, to Which Is Added the Original Epilogue*, Edinburgh, 1771.

———, *The Dramatic Works of Samuel Foote, Esq.*, 2 vols, London, 1797.

BIBLIOGRAPHY

Foote, Samuel, *A Letter from Mr Foote, to the Reverend Author of the Remarks, Critical and Christian on The Minor*, London, 1760.

———, *The Minor*, in *Modern British Drama*, London, 1811, V. 286–301.

Free, John, *A Sermon Preached before the University at St Mary's in Oxford, on Whitsunday 1758. With a Preface in Vindication of Certain Articles Proposed to the Serious Consideration of the Company of Salters in London: and an Appendix Containing Authentick Vouchers; from the Writings of the Methodists, etc., in Support of the Charge, Which Has Been Brought against Them*, 2nd edn, London, 1758.

G., T., *Remarks on the Reverend Mr Whitefield's Journal. Wherein His Many Inconsistences Are Pointed Out, and His Tenets Consider'd. The Whole Shewing the Dangerous Tendency of His Doctrine*, London, 1738.

Genuine and Secret Memoirs Relating to the Life and Adventures of That Arch Methodist, Mr G. W - - - fi - - d, Likewise, Critical and Explanatory Remarks upon that Inimitable Piece Entitled God's Dealings with the Rev. Mr Whitefield, Oxford, 1742.

Gib, Adam, *A Warning against Countenancing the Ministrations of Mr George Whitefield, Published in the New Church at Bristow, upon Sabbath, June 6, 1742. Together with an Appendix upon the Same Subject, Wherein Are Shewn, that Mr Whitefield Is No Minister of Jesus Christ; that His Call and Coming to Scotland Are Scandalous; that His Practice Is Disorderly, and Fertile of Disorder; that His Whole Doctrine Is, and His Success Must Be, Diabolical; so that People Ought to Avoid Him, from Duty to God, to the Church, to Themselves, to Fellow-Men, to Posterity, and to Him*, 2nd edn, Edinburgh, 1742.

[Gibson, Edmund] *An Earnest Appeal to the Publick; on Occasion of Mr Whitefield's Extraordinary Answer to the Pastoral Letter of the Lord Bishop of London. Intended to Vindicate His Lordship from the Extravagant Charges and Mean Evasions Contained in the Said Pretended Answer; and to Detect the True Spirit and Design of Its Author, from His Notorious Inconsistences with Himself, etc.*, London, 1739.

———, *Observations upon the Conduct and Behaviour of a Certain Sect Usually Distinguished by the Name of Methodists*, 3rd edn, London, 1744.

Goldsmith, Oliver. *The Miscellaneous Works of Oliver Goldsmith, Including a Variety of Pieces Now First Collected*. Ed. James Prior. 4 vols. Philadelphia, 1875.

———, *She Stoops to Conquer or The Mistakes of a Night*, ed. Katharine C. Balderston, New York, 1951.

Graves, Richard, *The Spiritual Quixote or, The Summer's Ramble of*

Mr Geoffrey Wildgoose, intro. Charles Whibley, 2 vols, London, 1926.

[Green, John] *The Principles and Practices of the Methodists Considered, in Some Letters to the Leaders of That Sect. The First Addressed to the Reverend Mr B[erridg]e Wherein Are Some Remarks on His Two Letters to a Clergyman in Nottinghamshire, Lately Published*, 2nd edn, London, 1761.

[————], *The Principles and Practices of the Methodists Farther Considered; in a Letter to the Reverend Mr George Whitefield*, Cambridge, 1761.

Green, Thomas, *A Dissertation on Enthusiasm, Shewing the Danger of Its Late Increase, and the Great Mischiefs It Has Occasioned, Both in Ancient and Modern Times, with an Examination of the Claims in General Now Laid to Immediate Revelations, Calls, Gifts, or Extraordinary Communications of the Spirit. Likewise Some Observations on the Most Distinguishing Traits of Our Modern Enthusiasts. To Which Is Added, by Way of Appendix, an Extract (with Some Additional Remarks) from Mr Rimius's Late Account of the Moravians, and Their Doctrines*, London, 1755.

[Grey, Zachary] *A Serious Address to Lay-Methodists, to Beware of the False Pretences of Their Teachers. With An Appendix Containing an Account of the Fatal and Bloody Effects of Enthusiasm; in the Case of the Family of the Dutartres, in South-Carolina. Which Was Attended with the Murder of Two Persons, and the Execution of Four for Those Murders*, London, 1745.

Gurney, Thomas, *Poems on Various Occasions*, Sudbury, 1790.

[Hardy, Richard] *A Letter from a Clergyman to One of His Parishioners, Who Was Inclined to Turn Methodist, with an Appendix Concerning the Means of Conversion, and the Imputation of Righteousness*, London, 1753.

Harman, John, *Remarks upon the Life, Character, and Behaviour of the Rev. George Whitefield, as Written by Himself, from the Time of His Birth, to the Time He Departed from His Tabernacle. Demonstrating, by Astronomical Calculation, that His Ascention, Meridinn, and Declination Were Necessarily Actuated by Planetary Influence; and that His Doctrine Was Not from Divine Mission, but from a Mere Fatality, Evident as Daily Seen in the Fatal Catastrophe of His Unhappy, Gloomy, and Misguided Followers. The Whole Being a Choice New Year's Gift for Methodists, and One of the Most Valuable Prizes That Ever Were Drawn for Methodists since Methodism Has Been in Being*, London, 1764.

Helton, John, *Reasons for Quitting the Methodist Society: Being a Defence of Barclay's Apology in Answer to a Printed Letter to a Person Joined with the People Called Quakers*, 3rd edn, Dublin printed, Philadelphia reprinted, 1784.

BIBLIOGRAPHY

Hill, R., *The Gospel-Shop, a Comedy of Five Acts; with a New Prologue and Epilogue, Originally Intended for Public Representation, but Suppressed at the Particular Desire of Some Eminent Divines* [London, 1778].

[Hill, Richard] *Goliath Slain: Being a Reply to the Reverend Dr Nowell's Answer to Pietas Oxoniensis. Wherein the False Glosses of That Gentleman's Pamphlet Are Removed, His Great Misrepresentations Detected, the Ancient Doctrines of the Reformation and of the Church of England Defended, and the Sentence against the Expelled Young Men Proved from His Own Words to Be Far More Severe, Arbitrary, and Illegal, Etc.*, London, 1768

[————] *Pietas Oxoniensis; or, A Full and Impartial Account of the Expulsion of Six Students from St Edmund Hall, Oxford*, London, 1768.

[————] *A Review of All the Doctrines Taught by the Rev. Mr John Wesley; Containing a Full and Particular Answer to a Book Entitled 'A Second Check to Antinomianism': in Six Letters to the Rev. Mr F - - r. Wherein the Doctrines of a Twofold Justification, Free Will, Man's Merit, Sinless Perfection, Finished Salvation, and Real Antinomianism Are Particularly Discussed, Etc.*, 2nd edn, London, 1772.

[————] *Some Remarks on a Pamphlet, Entitled, A Third Check to Antinomianism*, London, 1772.

Hill, Rowland, *A Full Answer to the Rev. J. Wesley's Remarks upon a Late Pamphlet, Published in Defence of the Characters of the Rev. Mr Whitefield and Others. In a Letter to a Friend*, Bristol [1777].

Hill, Rowland, *Imposture Detected, and the Dead Vindicated: in a Letter to a Friend Containing Some Gentle Strictures on the False and Libellous Harangue, Lately Delivered by Mr. John Wesley, upon His Laying the First Stone of His New Dissenting Meeting-House, near the City-Road*, London, 1777.

J., S., 'The Secret Disclosed; or, The Itinerant Field Orator's Methodist Gibberish; Lately Delivered in This Neighbourhood', *The Gentleman's Magazine*, LVIII (1788), pp. 488–9.

Jephson, Alexander, *A Friendly and Compassionate Address to All Serious and Well Disposed Methodists; in Which Their Principal Errors Concerning the Doctrine of the New Birth, Their Election and the Security of Their Salvation, and Their Notion of the Community of Christian Men's Goods, Are Largely Displayed and Represented*, London, 1760.

J - - ps - n, R - - ph, *The Expounder Expounded: or, Annotations upon That Incomparable Piece, Intitled, A Short Account of God's Dealings with the Rev. Mr G - - e W - - f - d. Wherein Several Profound Mysteries, Which Were Greatly Subject to Misconception,*

Are Set in a Clear Light; and the Abominable Secret Sin, Therein Mentioned, Is Particularly Illustrated and Explained, London, 1740.

Jerningham, *Enthusiasm: a Poem in Two Parts*, London, 1789.

Johnson, Samuel, *A Dictionary of the English Language: in Which the Words Are Deduced from their Originals; and Illustrated in Their Different Significations by Examples from the Best Writers. To Which Are Prefixed, a History of the Language, and an English Grammar*, London, 1852.

The Letters of Samuel Johnson, collected and edited by R. W. Chapman, Oxford, 1952.

Johnstone, Charles, *Chrysal or The Adventures of a Guinea*, ed. E. A. Baker, London, n.d.

A Journal of the Travels of Nathaniel Snip, a Methodist Teacher of the Word. Containing, an Account of the Many Marvellous Adventures Which Befel Him in His Way from the Town of Kingston upon Hull to the City of York, London, 1761.

Kirkby, John, *The Impostor Detected; or, The Counterfeit Saint Turn'd Inside Out*, London, 1750.

Lackington, James, *Memoirs of the First Forty-five Years of the Life of James Lackington*, London, 1791.

[Lancaster, Nathaniel] *Methodism Triumphant, or, The Decisive Battle between the Old Serpent and the Modern Saint*, London, 1767.

A Lash at Enthusiasm: in a Dialogue Founded upon Real Facts, between Mrs Clinker and Miss Martha Steady, Shrewsbury, n.d.

[Lavington, George] *The Bishop of Exeter's Answer to Mr J. Wesley's Late Letter to His Lordship*. London, 1752.

[————] *The Enthusiasm of Methodists and Papists Compar'd*, London, 1749.

'A Letter from a Mountebank Doctor to a Methodist Preacher,' *The Gentleman's Magazine, and Historical Chronicle*, XXVIII (1758), pp. 101-2.

A Letter of Expostulation from the Manager of the Theatre in Tottenham-Court, to the Manager of the Theatre in the Hay-Market. Relative to a New Comedy, Called The Minor, London, n.d.

A Letter to the Inhabitants of St Dunstan's in the West, Relating to Their Late Remarkable Proceeding with Regard to the Reverend Mr Romaine, Their Lecturer. With Some Remarks on Their Refusing Him Their Pulpit, and the Great Increase of Dissenters and Methodists, Fairly Stated, 2nd edn, London, 1759.

A Letter to the Reverend Mr George Whitefield, Occasioned by His Remarks upon a Pamphlet, Entitled The Enthusiasm of Methodists and Papists Compared, London, 1750.

A Letter to the Rev. Mr M - - re B - - k - r, Concerning the Methodists. By a Country-Gentleman, Dublin, 1752.

BIBLIOGRAPHY

[Lloyd, Evan] *The Methodist, a Poem*, London, 1766.
The Love-Feast. A Poem, London, 1778.
MacGowan, John, *The Foundry Budget Opened; or, The Arcanum of Wesleyanism Disclosed*, London, 1780.
———, *A Further Defence of Priestcraft; Being a Practical Improvement of the Shaver's Sermon on the Expulsion of Six Young Gentlemen from the University of Oxford, for Praying, Reading, and Expounding the Scriptures. Occasioned by a Vindication of That Pious Act by a Member of the University. Inscribed to Mr V - - C - - - and the H - - ds of H - - - s*, London, 1768.
[MacGowan, John] *Priestcraft Defended. A Sermon Occasioned by the Expulsion of Six Young Gentlemen from the University of Oxford, for Praying, Reading, and Expounding the Scriptures. Humbly Dedicated to Mr V - - - C - -- r and the Heads of H - - - s. By Their Humble Servant, the Shaver*, 7th edn, London printed, Boston reprinted, 1769.
[Madan, Martin] *An Exhortatory Address to the Brethren in the Faith of Christ, Occasioned by a Remarkable Letter from Mr Foote to the Rev. Author of Christian and Critical Remarks on The Minor. With a Serious Word or Two on the Present Melancholy Occasion. By a Minister of the Church of Christ*, London, 1760.
[Mason, William] *Methodism Displayed, and Enthusiasm Detected; intended as an Antidote against, and a Preservative from the Delusive Principles and Unscriptural Doctrines of a Modern Set of Seducing Preachers. And as a Defence of Our Regular and Orthodox Clergy, from Their Unjust Reflections. Address'd to the Rev. Mr Romaine, the Rev. Mr Jones, Etc.*, 3rd edn, London, 1757.
Methodism and Popery Dissected and Compared; and the Doctrines of Both Proved to Be Derived from a Pagan Origin; Including an Impartial and Candid Enquiry into the Writings of St Paul: with General Remarks on the Nature of, and Affinity between Enthusiasm and Superstition, London, 1779.
The Methodists, an Humorous Burlesque Poem: Address'd to the Rev. Mr Whitefield and His Followers: Proper to be Bound Up with His Sermons, and the Journals of His Voyage to Georgia, &c., London, 1739.
The Mock-Preacher: a Satyrico-Comical-Allegorical Farce. As It Was Acted to a Crowded Audience at Kennington-Common, and Many Other Theatres. With the Humours of the Mob, London, 1739.
[Moody, Robert] *Observations on Certain Prophecies in the Book of Daniel, and the Revelation of St John, Which Relate to the Second Appearing of Our Lord; Shewing That It Is Highly Probable that the Tremendous Day in Which He Shall Be Revealed Will Shortly Come. To Which Are Added Some Remarks Concerning the Last Anti-Christ and the Killing of the Witnesses*, London, 1787.

A New Letter to the Parishioners of St Dunstan's in the West, Relating to the Suspending the Reverend Mr Romaine. With a Sermon by the Reverend Mr D. Jones, London, 1759.

Nowell, Thomas, *An Answer to a Pamphlet, Entitled Pietas Oxoniensis, in a Letter to the Author Wherein the Grounds of the Expulsion of Six Members from St Edmund-Hall Are Set Forth; and the Doctrines of the Church of England, and Its First Reformers, Fully Considered and Vindicated*, 2nd edn, Oxford, 1769.

Observations and Remarks on Mr Seagrave's Conduct and Writings in Which His Answer to the Rev. Dr Trapp's Four Sermons Is More Particularly Considered, London, 1739.

'Observations on the Conduct of the Rev. Mr Whitefield, &c.', *Weekly Miscellany* (May 5, 12, 1739), reprinted in *The Gentleman's Magazine*, IX (1739), pp. 239–42.

O'Leary, Arthur, 'Remarks on the Rev. John Wesley's Letter, Concerning the Civil Principles of Roman Catholics. And a Defense of the Protestant Association', in O'Leary, *Miscellaneous Tracts on Several Interesting Subjects*, 3rd edn, London, 1791.

'On Reading Mr J. Wesley's Calm Address to the Inhabitants of England', *The Gospel Magazine, or Treasury of Divine Knowledge Designed to Promote Experimental Religion*, IV (1777), p. 226.

Owen, T. E., *Methodism Unmasked, or The Progress of Puritanism from the Sixteenth to the Nineteenth Century: Intended as an Explanatory Supplement to 'Hints to Heads of Families'*, London, 1802.

The Oxford Methodists: Being an Account of Some Young Gentlemen in That City, in Derision So Called; Setting Forth Their Rise and Designs, with Some Occasional Remarks on a Letter Inserted in Fog's Journal of December 9th, 1732, Relating to Them, 2nd edn, London, 1738.

Paragraph, Peter, *The Methodist and Mimick, a Tale in Hudibrastick Verse Inscribed to Samuel Foote, Esq.*, 2nd edn, London, 1767.

Perfection. A Poetical Epistle. Calmly Addressed to the Greatest Hypocrite in England, London, 1778.

A Plain Address to the Followers and Favourers of the Methodists, London, n.d.

A Plain and Easy Road to the Land of Bliss, a Turnpike Set Up by Mr Orator - -; on Which a Man May Travel More Miles in One Day, than on Any Other Highway in Forty Years. With a Dedication, Such as Never Was, or Will Be, in Vogue, London, 1762.

[Portal, Abraham] *A Letter to David Garrick, Esq.; Occasioned by the Intended Representation of The Minor at the Theatre-Royal in Drury-Lane*, 3rd edn, Edinburgh, 1770.

[Pottinger, Israel] *The Methodist, a Comedy, Being a Continuation and Completion of the Plan of The Minor, Written by Mr Foote*, 3rd edn, London [1761].

BIBLIOGRAPHY

The Question, Whether It Be Right to Turn Methodist, Considered in a Dialogue between Two Members of the Church of England, London, 1745.
Ranae Comicae Evangelizantes: or, The Comic Frogs Turned Methodist, London, 1786.
Reed, Joseph, *The Register-Office; a Farce in Two Acts,* new edn, London, 1771.
Reverend Doctor Westley's Dream, Being an Apology for His Fall, and His Late Pamphlet, &c. Also His Disciples Address in Consequence of His Dream and Admonitions, n.p., 1792.
Riley, William, *Parochial Music Corrected. Containing Remarks on the Performance of Psalmody in Country Churches, and on the Ridiculous and Profane Manner of Singing Practised by the Methodists; Reflections on the Bad Performance of Psalmody in London, Westminster, &c. With Some Hints for the Improvement of It in Public Worship; Observations on the Choice and Qualifications of Parish-Clerks; the Utility of Teaching Charity-Children Psalmody and Hymns, Etc.,* London, 1762.
A Satirical Dialogue between the Celebrated Mr F - - te, and Dr Squintum; as It Happened near the Great Lumber-House in Tottenham-Court Road, London, 1760.
'The Serpent and the Fox; or, An Interview between Old Nick and Old John', *The Gospel Magazine, or Treasury of Divine Knowledge Designed to Promote Experimental Religion,* IV (1777), pp. 330–1.
Shirley, Walter, *A Narrative of the Principal Circumstances Relative to the Rev. Mr Wesley's Late Conference Held in Bristol, August the 6th, 1771, at Which the Rev. Mr Shirley and Others, His Friends, Were Present, with the Declaration Then Agreed to by Mr Wesley, and Fifty-three of the Preachers in Connexion with Him,* Bath, 1771.
Sketches for Tabernacle-Frames. A Poem. By the Author of The Saints, a Satire; Perfection, &c., &c., London, 1778.
Smith, Haddon, *Methodistical Deceit: A Sermon Preached in the Parish Church of St Matthew, Bethnal Green, Middlesex; on the 29th of April, 1770,* London, 1770.
Smollett, Tobias, *The Works of Tobias Smollett,* intro. W. E. Henley, 12 vols, New York, 1899.
The Spiritual Minor, a Comedy, London, n.d.
[Sterne, Laurence] *A Funeral Discourse Occasioned by the Much Lamented Death of Mr Yorick, Prebendary of Y - - k and Author of the Much Admired Life and Opinions of Tristram Shandy, Preached before a Very Mixed Society of Jemmies, Jessamies, Methodists and Christians at a Nocturnal Meeting in Petticoat Lane and Now Published at the Unanimous Request of the Hearers*

by Christopher Flagellan, A.M., and Enriched with the Notes of Various Commentators. Aretopolis, the Capital of Eutopia, 1761.

Sterne, Laurence, *The Sermons of Mr Yorick*, Shakespeare Head edn, 2 vols, Oxford, 1927.

[Stevens, George Alexander] *The Celebrated Lecture on Heads; Which Has Been Exhibited Upwards of One Hundred Successive Nights to Crouded Audiences, and Met with the Most Universal Applause*, London, 1765.

The Story of the Methodist-Lady: or The Injur'd Husband's Revenge. A True History, London [1770].

A Supplement to the Rev. Mr Whitefield's Answer to the Bishop of London's Last Pastoral Letter Containing, I. Notes on the Pastoral Letter. II. A Remark on the Weekly Miscellany of August 18, 1739; with an Extract of a Letter from Mr Seward, Relating to the Writer of the Same, n.p., n.d.

T., R., 'On Mr Whitefield's Preaching', *The Gentleman's Magazine*, IX (1739), p. 323.

The Temple of Imposture; a Poem. By the Author of The Saints, a Satire, Perfection, &c., &c., London, 1778.

Toplady, Augustus M., *The Works of Augustus M. Toplady, A.B.*, new edn, 6 vols, London, 1825.

Tottie, John, *Two Charges Delivered to the Clergy of the Diocese of Worcester in the Years 1763 and 1766; Being Designed as Preservatives against the Sophistical Arts of the Papists, and the Delusions of the Methodists*, Oxford, 1766.

Transactions of the London Methodist Parsons. In Three Poetical Epistles, London, 1792.

Trapp, Joseph, *The Nature, Folly, Sin, and Danger of Being Righteous Over-Much; with a Particular View to the Doctrines and Practices of Certain Modern Enthusiasts*, London, 1739.

The True Spirit of the Methodists and Their Allies (Whether Other Enthusiasts, Papists, Deists, Quakers, or Atheists) Fully Laid Open, London, 1740.

Tucker, Josiah, *A Brief History of the Principles of Methodism, Wherein the Rise and Progress, Together with the Causes of the Several Variations, Divisions, and Present Inconsistencies of This Sect Are Attempted to Be Traced Out, and Accounted for*, Oxford, 1742.

[Tucker, Josiah] *A Compleat Account of the Conduct of That Eminent Enthusiast Mr Whitefield*, London, 1739.

'Verses Occasioned by the Bishop of London's Remarks upon Whit - - - d's Journals', *The London Magazine: and Monthly Chronologer* [VIII] (1739), pp. 621–2.

[Viney, Richard] *A Letter from an English Brother of the Moravian Persuasion to the Methodists in England, Lamenting the Irregularity of Their Present Proceedings*, London, 1739.

BIBLIOGRAPHY

Voltaire's Ghost to the Apostle of the Sinless Foundery: a Familiar Epistle from the Shades, London, 1779.
[Warne, Jonathan] *Dr Trapp Try'd and Cast; and Allowed to the 10th of May Next to Recant. Being Some Remarks on a Late Book, Intitled, The Nature, Folly, Sin, and Danger of Being Righteous Overmuch*, 2nd edn, London, 1739.
[————] *The Downfal of Arminianism; or Arminius (Who Falsly Calls Himself a Son of the Church of England.) Tried and Cast, (and in Him All His Adherents, Who Call Themselves Sons of the Church of England.) before the Right Honourable the Lord Chief Justice Truth, Etc.*, London, 1742.
The Journal of the Rev. John Wesley, A.M., ed. Nehemiah Curnock. 8 vols, London, 1938.
Woolley, W., *A Cure for Canting or, The Grand Imposters of St Stephen's and of Surrey Chapels Unmasked: in a Letter to Sir Richard Hill, Bart.*, London, 1794.

Secondary Bibliography

Baker, Eric W., *A Herald of the Evangelical Revival*, London, 1948.
Barr, Josiah Henry, *Early Methodists under Persecution*, New York, 1916.
Baugh, Albert C., ed. *A Literary History of England.* New York, 1948.
Belden, Albert D., *George Whitefield—The Awakener*, 2nd edn, London, 1953.
Belden, Mary Megie, *The Dramatic Works of Samuel Foote*, New Haven, 1929 (Yale Studies in English, LXXX).
Bond, Richmond P., *English Burlesque Poetry 1700-1750*, Cambridge 1932.
Bredvold, Louis I., 'A Note in Defence of Satire', *ELH*, VII (1940), pp. 253-64.
Cameron, Richard M., *The Rise of Methodism: A Sourcebook*, New York, 1954.
Carter, Henry, *The Methodist Heritage*, New York, 1951.
[Cavender, Curtis H.] *Catalogue of Works in Refutation of Methodism, from Its Origin in 1729, to the Present Time*, Philadelphia, 1846.
Church, Leslie F., *The Early Methodist People*, 2nd edn, London, 1949.
Clarke, W. K. Lowther, *Eighteenth Century Piety*, London, 1944.
Creed, John M., and J. S. Boys Smith, *Religious Thought in the Eighteenth Century*, Cambridge, 1934.
Dimond, Sydney G., *The Psychology of the Methodist Revival*, London, 1926.
Edwards, Maldwyn, *John Wesley and the Eighteenth Century*, London, 1933.

Elliott-Binns, L. E., *The Early Evangelicals: A Religious and Social Study*, London, 1953.
Ellis, Havelock, 'Richard Graves and "The Spiritual Quixote"', *Nineteenth Century and After*, LXXVII (1915), pp. 848–60.
Elton, Oliver, *A Survey of English Literature, 1730–80*, New York, 1928.
Fairchild, Hoxie N., *Religious Trends in English Poetry*, 3 vols, New York, 1939, 1942, 1949.
Fitzgerald, Percy, *Samuel Foote*, London, 1910.
Gill, Frederick C., *The Romantic Movement and Methodism*, London, 1937.
Gillies, John, *Memoirs of Rev. George Whitefield*, rev. edn, Middletown, 1838.
Green, Richard, *Anti-Methodist Publications Issued during the Eighteenth Century*, London, 1902.
Hartley, Lodwick, 'Cowper and the Polygamous Parson', *MLQ*, XVI (1955), pp. 137–41.
Hastings, James, ed., *Encyclopaedia of Religion and Ethics*, 13 vols, New York, 1951.
Herbert, Thomas Walter, *John Wesley as Editor and Author*, Princeton, 1940. (Princeton Studies in English No. 17.)
Henry, Stuart C., *George Whitefield: Wayfaring Witness*, New York, 1957.
Hill, Charles Jarvis, *The Literary Career of Richard Graves*, Northampton, 1935. (Smith College Studies in Modern Language, Vol. XVI, Nos. 1–3.)
Jack, Ian, *Augustan Satire: Intention and Idiom in English Poetry, 1660–1750*, Oxford, 1952.
Jackson, Thomas, *The Life of the Rev. Charles Wesley, M.A.*, New York, 1842.
King, C. Harold, 'God's Dramatist', *Studies in Speech and Drama in Honor of Alexander M. Drummond*, Ithaca, 1944.
Knox, Ronald A., *Enthusiasm, a Chapter in the History of Religion*, New York, 1951.
Lam, George L., and Warren H. Smith, 'Two Rival Editions of George Whitefield's *Journal*, London, 1738', *SP*, XLI (1944), pp. 86–93.
Lecky, W. E. H., *A History of England in the Eighteenth Century*, new edn, New York, 1892.
Lee, Umphrey, *The Historical Backgrounds of Early Methodist Enthusiasm*, New York, 1931.
——, *The Lord's Horseman*, New York, 1954.
Lunn, Arnold, *John Wesley*, New York, 1929.
Mack, Maynard, 'The Muse of Satire', *Yale Review*, XLI (1951), pp. 80–92.

Ong, Walter J., 'Peter Ramus and the Naming of Methodism: Medieval Science through Ramist Homiletic', *JHI*, XIV (1953), pp. 235-48.
Shepherd, T. B., *Methodism and the Literature of the Eighteenth Century*, 2nd edn, London, 1947.
———, 'Methodists and the Theatre in the Eighteenth Century', *Proceedings of the Wesley Historical Society*, XX (1935-6), pp. 166-8, 181-5, XXI (1937-8), pp. 3-7.
Stephen, Leslie, *English Literature and Society in the Eighteenth Century*, New York, 1907.
———, *History of English Thought in the Eighteenth Century*, reprint edn, 2 vols, London, 1927.
Stromberg, Roland N., *Religious Liberalism in Eighteenth-Century England*, London, 1954.
Sutherland, James, *Background for Queen Anne*, London, 1939.
———, *A Preface to Eighteenth-century Poetry*, Oxford, 1948, 1950.
Townsend, W. J., H. B. Workman, and George Eayrs, eds, *A New History of Methodism*, 2 vols, Nashville, n.d.
Tyerman, Luke, *The Life and Times of the Rev. John Wesley, M.A., Founder of the Methodists*, 6th edn, 3 vols, London, 1890.
———, *The Life of the Rev. George Whitefield*, 2 vols, London, 1876-7.
Warner, Wellman J., *The Wesleyan Movement in the Industrial Revolution*, London, 1930.
Whelan, M. Kevin, *Enthusiasm in English Poetry of the Eighteenth Century (1700-74)*, Washington, 1935.
Whiteley, J. H., *Wesley's England*, reprint edn, London, 1945.
Wilkinson, Andrew M., 'The Decline of English Verse Satire in the Middle Years of the Eighteenth Century', *RES*, III (1952), pp. 222-33.
——— 'The Rise of English Verse Satire in the Eighteenth Century', *English Studies*, XXXIV (1953), pp. 97-108.
Willey, Basil, *The Eighteenth-century Background*, London, 1946.
Williams, Aubrey L., *Pope's Dunciad: A Study of Its Meaning*, Baton Rouge, 1955.

Index

Absalom and Achitophel, 32
Absence of sin in the elect, 47, 54, 55–7
Account of God's Dealings with the Reverend Mr George Whitefield, 99, 130, 131, 132–3
Anstey, Christopher, 109
Antinomianism, 26–8, 44, 46, 49, 54, 58, 61, 127
Anti-thelyphthora, 147
Apology for the Life of Mrs Shamela Andrews, An, 50
Arminianism, 46, 47–8, 58–60, 116
Arrogance, spiritual, of Methodists, 149, 150, 156–7, 163
Articles of Religion, 26, 44, 47, 154
Assurance, 26, 28, 47, 54–5, 61

Bedford, Arthur, 55
Beecher, Michael, 158
Bennett, John, 141
Benson, Martin, 155n
Berridge, John, 48, 49
Bickerstaff, Isaac, 65, 68, 77, 159n, 161
Booker, Moore, 139, 142–3
Borough, The, 11, 78, 154–5
Boswell, James, 85n, 121n
Bowden, Samuel, 21, 56–7
Bull, Patrick, 123, 124
Butler, Samuel, 16, 111

Calm Address to Our American Colonies, A, 19, 112, 119, 120–4, 127, 167, 169
Calvinist Methodists and Methodism, 15, 18, 19, 23, 45n, 46, 47, 50, 55–6, 58–60, 66n, 86, 112, 114n, 116, 117, 139, 140, 143–7, 154, 157
Carey, Henry, 29
Celebrated Lecture on Heads, The, 75–6, 81, 130, 135n

Chatterton, Thomas, 93
Christian Library, 87
Christian Perfection, 148
Chrysal, 135
Church of England, 149–163; attacks upon Anglican clergy, 153–6; clergy as satirists of Methodism, 17, 18, 30; Methodists as members of, 149, 150, 151–3; Methodist belief in doctrines of, 24, 27, 44–6, 150; Methodists causing dissension in, 26–8; Methodist separation from, 151–2
Conference between a Mystic, an Hutchinsonian, a Calvinist, a Methodist, a Member of the Church of England, and Others, A, 28n
Confession, 88–9
Conventicle Act, 11, 18, 75
Conversion, 76, 79–80, 81, 85, 96–110, 149, 156
Converts, 96–101
Coventry, Francis, 100, 133
Cowper, William, 147
Crabbe, George, 11, 78, 154
Cromwell, Oliver, 30, 32
Cumberland, Richard, 50, 56, 76, 79n
Cure for Canting, A, 72n, 74n, 144n

Delamotte, Charles, 82, 83n
Devil upon Two Sticks, The, 16, 69
Dissertation on Enthusiasm, A, 95
Doctrine, lack of, 46, 47, 60–1
Dodd, William, 28, 63
Downes, John, 22, 23, 46, 47, 48
Drugs, use of, 105, 115, 119
Dryden, John, 32, 111, 116
Dunciad, The, 148, 164, 171

Earnest and Affectionate Address to the People Called Methodists, An, 15, 47, 93, 94n

187

INDEX

Enthusiasm, 32–8, 38–43, passim
Enthusiasm of Methodists and Papists Compar'd, The, 18, 94n, 104, 158
Erasmus, Bishop of Arcadia, 124–5
Essay Concerning Human Understanding, 33
Evangelicals, 22
Evans, Theophilus, 56, 76, 104, 107
Expounder Expounded, The, 128, 130, 131, 133n, 134, 166

Fanatic Saints, The, 55, 58, 65, 74, 80, 86n, 89n, 122, 145, 146, 168n
Fanatical Conversion, 86n, 89n, 105, 119, 125, 165, 167, 170
Faulkner, George, 129
Fielding, Henry, 50, 99, 131, 133
Field preaching, 15, 18, 62, 75–6, 82, 96, 127, 148, 165
Fine Picture of Enthusiasm, A, 35, 45n, 78, 92, 152
Fletcher, John, 142
Fogg's Weekly Journal, 11, 15, 82n
Foote, Samuel, 16, 40, 52, 53, 64, 69, 98, 101, 111, 128, 129, 137, 143, 157, 160–1, 168n
Foundry Budget Opened, The, 60
Franklin, Benjamin, 135
Free, John, 78, 84
French Prophets, 32, 111
Friendly and Compassionate Address to All Serious and Well Disposed Methodists, A, 154
Funeral Discourse Occasioned by the Much Lamented Death of Mr Yorick, A, 66n, 89–90

Garrick, David, 143, 156
Gentlemen's Magazine, The, 69n, 93, 109
Genuine and Secret Memoirs Relating to the Life and Adventures of That Arch Methodist, Mr G. W—fi—d, 128n, 165n
Gibson, Edmund, 63, 152, 153n
Goldsmith, Oliver, 72, 73, 74
Gospel Magazine, The, 122
Graves, Richard, 16, 21, 28, 34, 51–2, 54, 68, 72, 75, 78, 80, 86, 87, 131, 148, 160, 167, 170

Green, John, 37
Green, Thomas, 95
Grimshaw, William, 159
Gurney, Thomas, 59

Hall, Westley, 141
Hardy, Richard, 48
Harman, John, 27, 100, 113, 131
Harris, Howell, 148
Henry, 50, 56, 76, 79, 167
Herrnhut, 125, 148
Hervey, James, 120n
Hill, Richard, 45n, 47, 58, 59, 139, 140, 144
Hill, Rowland, 18, 59, 74n, 139, 140, 144–5, 152, 153n
History of Pompey the Little, 100n, 133, 169
Holy Club, 22, 82, 87, 93, 150
Holy Communion, 93–4, 95n, 151–2
Hopkey, Sophia, 86, 114
Hudibras, 16, 164
Humphrey Clinker, 38, 51, 85, 103, 167
Huntingdon, Countess of, 96, 143–4
Hymns and hymn-singing, 82, 85, 86, 91–3, 107, 120
Hypocrisy, 26, 28–9, 32, 38, 76, 159–60, 171
Hypocrite, The, 65, 69, 159, 161, 168n

Imposter Detected, The, 35, 78, 140
Ingham, Benjamin, 82, 83n, 140
Inspiration, 33–9, 72, 149–50, 154–5
Itineration, 75, 96, 127

Jephson, Alexander, 154
Johnson, James, 155n
Johnson, Samuel, 20, 33, 81, 85n, 112, 121–3
Johnstone, Charles, 135
Jones, Griffith, 147–8
Jones, Thomas, 147
Joseph Andrews, 133
Journal of a Tour to the Hebrides, 121
Journal of the Travels of Nathaniel Snip, 39, 41, 51, 66, 75, 76, 77, 79, 80, 87, 99, 138, 154, 157, 167, 168

INDEX

Journals, keeping of, 82, 83–4, 95, 167
Justification by faith, 18, 26–7, 45, 46–54, 58, 61, 99, 116, 127
Justification by Faith Alone, 49

Kirkby, John, 35, 61, 78n, 92, 140

Lackington, James, 26, 40, 52, 56, 67, 71, 83, 85, 86, 87, 89, 97, 100, 103, 107, 108, 133, 151, 156, 158, 159, 166
Lancaster, Nathaniel, 42, 77, 87, 97, 99, 100, 106, 108, 114, 115, 120, 155, 156, 157, 158, 161
Language, Methodist, 62, 70, 77–81, 133–5, 157
Launcelot Greaves, 54
Lavington, George, 17, 94, 104, 105, 133, 158
Law, William, 57, 148
Lay preachers and lay preaching, 15–16, 27–8, 39, 48, 51, 62–9, 75, 82–9, 149–50, 151, 167, 168, 170
Letter from Mr Foote, A, 39n, 40, 64n, 109n
Letter of Expostulation from the Manager of the Theatre in Tottenham-Court, A, 52, 101n, 165
Letter to the Inhabitants of St Dunstan's in the West, A, 24
Letter to the Reverend Mr George Whitefield, A, 23, 70, 148
Letter to the Rev. Mr M—re B—k—r, 36n, 92n, 94, 95, 105, 109, 142
Lloyd, Evan, 64, 129, 144, 146
Lloyd's Morning Post, 120, 125
Locke, John, 33, 36, 37
London Magazine, The, 71n, 84n, 108n, 154n
Lots, drawing of, 86
Love-Feast, The, 90, 92, 98, 100, 113, 119, 125, 140, 143, 145, 168n, 169
Love-feasts, 82, 89, 91, 95, 170
Luther, Martin, 102
Lyar, The, 16

MacFlecknoe, 111, 116, 164
MacGowan, John, 18, 60, 66n
Madan, Martin, 16, 139, 145, 146–7, 148, 160–1

Madness, Methodist, 25, 36, 38–9, 42–3, 54, 68, 70, 71–2, 92–3, 108–10, 157
Maxfield, Thomas, 62, 102, 104n, 147n
'Mechanic Inspir'd, The', 21
Melchizedekians, 15
Memoirs of the First Forty-five Years of the Life of James Lackington, 52
Methodism and Popery Dissected and Compared, 29, 117, 147
Methodism Displayed, 24
Methodism Examined and Disposed, 22, 46
Methodism Triumphant, 42, 70, 77, 87, 97, 100, 109, 114, 115, 120, 126, 148, 155, 157, 159, 161, 167n, 169, 171
Methodist, a Comedy, The, 16, 53, 69, 129, 161
Methodist and Mimick, The, 30, 129n
Methodist, a Poem, The, 27, 43n, 64, 67, 69, 129, 144, 146, 168n, 169, 171
Methodist, origin of name, 21–5, 30–1, 84
'Methodist Parson, The', 29
Methodists, an Humorous Burlesque Poem, The, 61, 70, 85, 97, 135, 137, 138, 152, 169
Methodists Dissected, The, 128
Milton, John, 16, 111, 169
Minor, The, 16, 19, 52, 53, 80, 98, 99, 128–9, 143, 160, 165
Mock Preacher, The, 17n, 19, 68n, 97, 135, 136, 165
Monthly Review, 17
Moravians, 22n, 55, 71, 83n, 86, 87, 89, 125n, 140, 148
Morgan, William, 82n
Murray, Alexander, 141
Murray, Grace, 114, 141–2, 148

Nature, Folly, Sin, and Danger of Being Righteous Overmuch, The, 17, 130n, 133n
New Bath Guide, The, 109
New Birth, 46, 64, 70, 71, 77, 79–80, 90, 103, 104, 105, 107, 109
Newton, John, 147

INDEX

Oratorical reform, 72–4
Orators, The, 16, 129, 168n

Paragraph, Peter, 30, 129, 137
Perfection, 57, 89n, 91, 115n, 121, 122, 125, 156, 166, 168n
Perfection, 26, 28, 45, 46, 47, 54, 57–8, 61, 86, 98, 114, 115, 119, 169
Perronet, Vincent, 142
Plain Address to the Followers and Favourers of the Methodists, A, 128
Plain and Easy Road to the Land of Bliss, A, 39, 41, 50, 67, 76, 89, 98, 99, 103, 106, 108, 117, 136, 140, 148n
Playhouses, attendance at, 17, 161–2, 163
Pope, Alexander, 16, 19, 20, 111, 132n
Pottinger, Israel, 16, 53, 129
Praying over sick, 87–8
Primitive Physick, 118
Principles and Practices of the Methodists Considered, The, 37n, 40
Puritans, 29, 32

Question, Whether It Be Right to Turn Methodist, The, 55

Ranae Comicae Evangelizantes, 97, 98n, 168n
Reason, denigration of, 38, 41–2, 154
Reed, Joseph, 16, 79n, 128
Register-Office, The, 16, 79, 128n, 167n
Regularity of life, 22, 26, 82
Review of all the Doctrines Taught by the Rev. Mr John Wesley, A, 58n, 94, 120
Riley, William, 93
Rochester, Earl of, 153
Romaine, William, 114n, 139, 145, 146
Roman Catholicism, 17, 30, 60, 61, 88–9, 94–5, 137, 152, 169

Satire, defined, 11; extent of, 18–19; principles of Augustan, 19–21

Satirical Dialogue between the Celebrated Mr F—te, and Dr Squintum, 135n, 144n, 157
Satirists, aims, purposes, and motivations of, 19–21, 25–6, 164–7
Serious Address to Lay-Methodists, A, 73
Serious Call to a Devout and Holy Life, A, 148
Sermon Preached before the University at St Mary's in Oxford, on Whitsunday, 1758, A, 78n, 84
Sexual immorality, 53–4, 58, 68, 69–71, 89–91, 99, 125, 126, 131–2, 137, 167, 168
Shadwell, Thomas, 111
She Stoops to Conquer, 74
Shirley, Walter, 23, 59
Sketches for Tabernacle-Frames, 29, 71, 73, 107n, 113, 118, 122, 132, 157n
Smollett, Tobias, 38, 54, 167
Societies, Methodist, 86–7, 88, 151, 152, 160
Spiritual Minor, The, 16, 53, 97, 129, 135, 161
Spiritual Quixote, The, 16, 21, 28, 34, 51, 54, 68, 72, 75n, 78n, 80, 86, 131, 160, 167
Sterne, Laurence, 66, 89–90
Stevens, George Alexander, 130n
Story of the Methodist-Lady, The, 106, 108, 166
Swift, Jonathan, 16, 19, 35, 39, 50, 109, 111

Tale of a Tub, A, 39, 50, 164
Taxation No Tyranny, 112, 121, 122, 123
Taylor, Jeremy, 83
Temple of Imposture, The, 113n, 116, 146, 167, 169
Thelyphthora, 146
Toleration Act, 151
Tom Jones, 131
Toplady, Augustus, 18, 59, 120, 122, 124, 125, 139, 140, 147
Tottie, John, 104
Transubstantiation, 94

INDEX

Trapp, Joseph, 17, 20, 33, 37, 63, 130n, 133n, 153n
Trevecca College, 143, 151n

Vazeille, Mrs Molly, 114
Venn, Henry, 142
Voltaire's Ghost to the Apostle of the Sinless Foundery, 114, 120n, 122n, 125, 141, 147, 168n

Waller, James, 30
Warburton, William, 155
Watch-night services, 82, 89, 90–1, 95, 170
Watts, Isaac, 92
Weekly Miscellany, 17
Wesley, Charles, 15, 30, 77n, 84, 92, 95n, 114, 119, 136, 139, 140, 141
Wesley, John, 15, 16, 17, 18, 19, 22, 25, 28, 34, 35, 40, 42, 44–6, 48, 49, 54–6, 57–8, 59, 60, 61, 62–3, 66–7, 73, 74, 75, 76, 77, 83, 84, 86, 87, 88, 90, 91, 92, 93, 94, 96, 101–2, 104, 105, 107, 111–26, 127, 128, 138, 139, 140, 141–2, 148, 150, 151, 152–3, 157–8, 160–1, 168; *Journal*, 34n, 35, 40, 45, 54, 55n, 75, 83, 85n, 86n, 87, 88n, 90n, 102, 119–20, 141n, 147, 150, 153n, 157, 160
Wheatley, James, 147
Whitefield, George, 15, 16, 17, 18, 19, 23, 27, 28, 37, 39, 40, 44, 52, 53, 55, 68, 69, 75, 76, 80, 83, 86, 97, 99, 100, 101, 102, 112–13, 114, 117, 127–38, 139, 140, 143, 144, 148, 153, 156, 157, 158, 160, 161, 165, 166, 168; *Journals*, 127, 132–3
Whole Duty of Man, The, 87, 158
Wolf in Sheep's Cloathing, A, 123, 169
Wooley, W., 72n, 74, 144

Zanchius, 120
Zinzendorf, Count, 148